THE UNSPOKEN RULES OF GETTING HIRED

107 Job Hunting Secrets

That Employers <u>Do NOT</u> Want You To Know

LANDON LONG

JESSE STRETCH

www.InterviewMasterMind.com

Grateful acknowledgement is made to Eben Pagan for his commitment to influencing the lives of others and changing the world with his teachings. Your work has guided and inspired me throughout this process. I am forever a fan and indebted to you.

This book couldn't have been written without my brilliant intern, Zach Elbert. Thank you for meeting deadlines and keeping me in check. I encourage all employers to hire you before their competition does!

For more information on our other products and services, visit
www.InterviewMasterMind.com

ISBN: 1-4392-5478-8
ISBN-13: 978-1439254783

Printed in the United States of America

Second Edition

For my family,

GRACE, JIMMY, AND MY GRANDMOTHER;

who taught a little hellion that the only thing standing

between you and your dreams is yourself.

I love you all and owe you everything.

And for my future wife DJ,

The special woman in my life,

who gave me unwavering support through the

ups and downs of writing this book.

I love you with all my heart.

TABLE OF CONTENTS

EDUCATION IS WHAT REMAINS
AFTER ONE HAS FORGOTTEN
EVERYTHING HE LEARNED
IN SCHOOL.

. . . .

—ALBERT EINSTEIN
Theoretical Physicist and 1921 Nobel Prize Winner

Dear Reader,

People like us didn't start off with a silver spoon in our mouths. Or, if we did, the silver spoon was taken away at one point or another. That's why you're here, reading this, trying to figure out how to safely and successfully navigate the seemingly indecipherable labyrinth known as Corporate America.

I take it that you don't have a job, or that you have a job that you don't like. This is the case for many people, and for many people this will continue to be the case for the next 30 years. Rest assured, this will not be the case for you. That is, if you are dedicated to your dreams, and thereby dedicated to your path of achieving massive success and comfort in your life. You can get any job you want, make any decision you choose, go in any direction imaginable. However, you must first choose a direction and a goal, and then acquire the skills and knowledge to take you there.

That being said, I have put together this book—a story of how I came to be called *The Interview Mastermind*—as a means of explaining the path I took to free myself from the cold shackles of unemployment. It is my sincere hope that my story, told from the perspective of a young man named Adrian Addler, will shed light on your current situations, both financial and personal, and will aid in your transformation, whatever it may be.

For some of you, the difficultly has arisen in finding a job. For others it has come about due to the need for finding a better job—a job you like, a job that pays more or that has better benefits. Whatever the case may be, the process of finding the job you want starts with how you present yourself. And I'd bet my ass you're not presenting yourself in the best light.

–Landon Long
Founder of **InterviewMasterMind.com**

MEET ADRIAN

My philosophies about life, getting a job, and being a happy person exploded mid-air when I was on the cusp of finishing college.

"You're a simple kind of guy, Adrian," my friends would tell me. "You make good grades and you're easy to get along with. You'll do fine. You'll get a good job. Don't worry about it."

These were the sons of executives or VPs. They were the kids who drove brand-new Beamers and flipped girlfriends like bad stock. They were my friends, but they were not me. I came from a modest family. My parents were nestled somewhere in the middle of middle-class America. My mother kept a secretarial position at a local glass-manufacturing company, and my father had been employed with R. Jamison Construction, a medium-sized general-contracting firm, for the past 25 years.

At the beginning of this story, I am 22 years old. I am an average-looking guy, and resemble a slightly more attractive version of Zac Efron. Although, some of my friends insist that this comparison is incorrect, that I'm merely a more mature-looking version of Jason Biggs—but what do they know? *Haters...*

I measure six feet tall, thin but not skinny, thick brown hair, clean shaven, and my body is constantly sore from hitting the gym for the first time in several years. I have no girlfriend and no job.

My name is Adrian Addler, and I am on my own.

*   *   *

My professors told me that my good grades would get me a good job. Of course they did. They were college professors; they wanted me to do well in their classes. They wanted to "teach" and they wanted me to "learn." Who cared if what I was learning would *really* apply to my life post-graduation? No one did. That was the problem. Unfortunately, I did not realize this.

I took the whole college experience with a smile on my face. I kept my grades up, made friends, hung out on the weekends, and did what was expected of me. I was a nice guy by nature, never had to fake too many smiles or tell too many lies. People told me that I had a great ability to get along with the world, and that the world would smile on me in the future.

People like to do that. They like to build you up and pat your back. Don't ask me why, but everyone assured me that I was "something special," that one day they would see me on the cover of the *Wall Street Journal* or *Forbes* magazine. And, to be quite honest, up until my last semester of college, I was stupid enough to believe them.

*   *   *

An old saying comes to mind: Hindsight is 20/20.

In hindsight, I could tell you about every hour that I wasted listening to a professor run his mouth about pointless shit. I could tell you every failed attempt I made at getting hired. I could tell you how many times I depended on the wrong people for the wrong guidance at the wrong time. I could tell you all of this, but it wouldn't change anything for you. You'd still do everything the wrong way. So, instead of focusing on the wrong, instead of wrecking the institutions you are probably already a part of, I will tell you how to beat those institutions, to beat the competition, and to make something of yourself in spite of having been held back by years of failed attempts at real-world education.

*   *   *

Let's start at the beginning, when I began to think about this stuff...

I was at square one: Jobless. Broke. Tired. A senior in college. Regardless of whether or not you went to college, we have all been unemployed at one point or another. Being unemployed, depending on who you are, is not necessarily a problem. Some people are entirely fine with making absolutely no money and living off their parents' funds. They always called me a simple guy, but I wasn't quite that simple.

I watched several of my older friends take the high road, and several take the low, and I figured that I'd rather be on the high side for reasons of health, comfort, and sanity.

I didn't realize it at the time, but by aiming for the high road, I had signed up to climb the tallest cliff in the world...without a tether. Like I said, I didn't have a CEO for a father, someone who could talk me through the whole "job market and finances" thing. I didn't have a trust fund to float me while I sent out three million résumés. I didn't have a girlfriend to hold me at night. I slept alone, beneath stringy spider webs and a pale white ceiling, and made up elaborate scenarios for my prosperous future.

Prosperous... I was far from it. I was driving a 17-year-old hunk of shit and eating dollar value meals at least once a day. I was living in a two-bedroom apartment with a beautiful woman who was NOT my girlfriend but who was successful, intelligent, and the desire of nearly every man within a 10-mile radius. It was a strange and unmapped world, and I was navigating it poorly at best.

*   *   *

As I have mentioned, senior year in college was my turning point. It was then that I realized the ultimate purpose of school: to become qualified and prepared for a specific job. This hadn't occurred to me before, and no one had really explained it in concrete terms. When it came time to get out there and start working, my job searches trembled at the knees and fell face-first into the dirt.

I come from a good family. My parents are good people, and they taught me how to act in public, how to speak, how to work hard and do well in school. Sadly, they had assumed that high school and college would teach me the rest—namely, how to get a job and become a learned and successful human being. Upon realizing that this was not the case, I called my dad and asked him what he knew about getting a job.

He laughed and said, "Son, I haven't applied for a job in 25 years. I have no idea what to do." Then he said something that killed me: "Didn't you pay attention in college?"

*   *   *

People assured me that I was doing OK.

"Adrian, you have an internship under your belt and you make good grades. You're an employer's dream. You should just relax. Things will be fine, you'll see..."

Somehow my grades kept coming up in these conversations. This always reinforced me, gave me the false strength I needed to push forward.

So, I did what most guys do: I lay in my bed at night and imagined the future. I had a nice house, a couple of kids, a golden retriever running through the yard, health insurance, a sailboat, a Maserati, another house overlooking South Beach (or some exotic location), a couple million in the bank, Heidi Klum wrapping her arms around me, giggling, whispering into my ear, sipping martinis...

Don't act like you haven't done this.

My friends' assurances did the worst thing possible: They kept me in my comfort zone. They allowed me to keep dreaming, knowing that after I graduated things would "work themselves out." It was when I first came into contact with the real world, when I first tried to get a job, that I realized the truth: You are on your own, always and indefinitely. You are your own person, and you must use every resource you have to achieve your goals.

SHOULD YOU FIND YOURSELF IN A CHRONICALLY LEAKING BOAT, ENERGY DEVOTED TO CHANGING VESSELS IS LIKELY TO BE MORE PRODUCTIVE THAN ENERGY DEVOTED TO PATCHING LEAKS.

. . . .

—WARREN BUFFET,
The Richest Person in the World, Forbes Magazine (2008)

CHAPTER 1

THE SUICIDE CALLER

An explosion occurred somewhere in my brain and I snapped awake, grabbing my wallet from the nightstand. I flipped it open to check for cash. Nothing. I had no more money. I rolled over and stared at the wall.

Last night I had been hanging out with my best friend, Jake Holland. There had been a bar, a girl, and several friends. I could remember it well: The girl's name was Isabelle and she had given me her phone number. Her friends had dragged her away from me at 2 a.m., just as the bar was closing.

My head pounded loudly, each heartbeat like a hammer on my skull. The daylight warmed the bedspread. I checked the alarm clock, which was still screaming: 10:07 a.m.

The house was too bright. I was hung over, tired, dehydrated, broke. I didn't want to move. The economy was in a tailspin, and I had no reason to believe that getting out of bed would have any sort of positive impact on the rest of my life.

"Alright," I said, stretching my arms and putting aside my negative emotions. "Time to get up."

I stumbled down the stairs and poured a glass of water. The bills were mounting and the bar tab from last night would surely overdraft my bank account. I'd subconsciously known this as I had been buying the drinks, but I'd bought them anyway.

I sat down at the counter and rubbed my temples. I stared at the screen like a hypnotized zombie, tapping my fingers on the space key and muttering to myself.

"Come on… come on…"

Several painful moments passed while I stared into the endless circle of *Loading... Loading... Loading...*

The morning would never amount to anything if my laptop crashed. Again.

I sat back and sighed, remembering Isabelle and running my fingers through my hair. I leaned back farther, farther, farther, until the chair came close to slipping out from beneath me.

I scrambled and caught myself on the table.

"Nice one, klutz," Emily, my roommate, said. She hopped down the last three stairs and entered the kitchen in a pair of sweatpants and a t-shirt.

Emily took a seat across from me and opened her laptop. We sat face to face, our computers pressed against each other at the breakfast table. Emily was a very close friend of mine. She was two years older than I was and had become a very successful recruiter for Harrell-Finch.

"How's it going?" I asked, my computer finally deciding to wake up.

"Good, good... I was out at Century Lounge last night," she said. "Talk about socializing with people who literally *stink* of too much money."

"Wow," I said. "I wouldn't mind smelling like that."

"I'm not complaining. I got to meet some really interesting people. It's just that I sometimes miss when you and I used to go out together. Now that I'm with Josh, it's like we don't hang out quite as much." She clicked something on her computer.

"Eh, it's OK. That's how it goes." I checked my Facebook page and noticed three new friend requests. There was some guy named Joe, another named Mickey, and then a girl I didn't know. Wait—I *did* know her. It was Isabelle, the girl from last night at the bar. I clicked the image. Man, she was gorgeous...

Emily walked around me and reached into the refrigerator. I quickly navigated back to my own profile to avoid having to answer any questions about Isabelle. Emily poured a glass of orange juice and walked up behind me.

"Have any luck with callbacks from your résumés?"

"No," I said. "I've been out there all week putting myself in the line of fire. I've been dropping off résumés, calling to see who is hiring and who would be a good company to work for. I'm starting to feel really unmotivated, like I'm not sure—"

She cut me off: "What is THAT?" she asked, slapping her finger against my screen.

I pushed her wrist away and shrugged my shoulders. "What are you talking about?"

"Is that a picture of you with... two forties taped to your hands?"

"Yeah," I chuckled. "It was the Edward Forty-Hand competition. I won this year."

"Jeez, Adrian..." She stepped back around the table, taking a long sip of her orange juice. "You've got to get rid of that picture. Almost all employers are now doing internet searches on their applicants. I was reading in *Marie Claire* that a woman just lost her job over something she said on Twitter."

"That's crazy," I said disapprovingly. "What did she say?"

"She said her job was boring and that the commute was too long. They rescinded the offer and took her job before she officially started."

"Wow," I said. "I didn't ever think about that."

"Maybe your employers aren't calling you back because they've seen the Edward Forty-Hands picture."

"Well, I doubt it, but I'll take it down anyway."

"Speaking of employers," Emily said, closing her laptop, "I heard you talking about Empyrean this morning. Are you putting in an application?"

"Yeah... I'm taking it as a sign that since I haven't gotten a single callback from 40 applications, I must be doing something wrong. Empyrean's accepting applications starting in April. I'm going to spend a little time tonight trying to revamp my résumé. I have three months to prepare for this job."

"Why don't you do a little research about the company tonight? Tomorrow, after I get back from Josh's art show, I'll help you write a good résumé. By the way, how's your cover letter coming along?"

"Well," I said, somewhat apprehensive about receiving unsolicited advice. "I don't know if that's really necessary. I think I can handle everything." I closed my Facebook page, having replaced my profile picture. "And honestly, I don't think a cover letter is really necessary in the first place."

"What? Are you serious!?" Emily looked flabbergasted.

"No one writes them anymore. Employers just throw your cover letter in the trash and go straight to the résumé."

"I wish you knew how untrue that really is…"

"What do you mean?" I asked. "Almost everybody agrees that they're a thing of the past."

"Says who? Jake? A cover letter is not only extremely important for reasons of professional presentation, it is also essential for promoting yourself."

"Promoting myself?"

"Yeah. Think of a cover letter as your promotional team. It's what promotes you from a distance since you're not physically able to do it yourself. The promotional team is tasked with getting the employer interested in your résumé. The cover letter should therefore lure the employers into reading your résumé by showing them your assertive personality."

"OK…" I said.

"And please, Adrian, don't crank out a dry, stilted, generic cover letter like most college grads do. You have no idea how bad they usually are. Every cover letter I read is as boring as a chemistry textbook and was clearly written as a one-size-fits-all document. It makes the candidate sound really predictable and boring.

"When 500 people apply to a company, only one or two get hired. People don't realize how crucial it is to put in a little bit of extra effort to find out how to make their approach *seem* even more personal. You know, things like finding out who to address your cover letter to before sending it out. Employers and recruiters pay particular attention to little details like that. It's the details that make the difference in landing more interviews. There is nothing I hate more than receiving a cover letter that starts with 'To Whom it May Concern' or 'Dear Sir or Madam.' It's so unprofessional."

"What do you mean? People don't get interviewed because they don't know who to address their cover letters to?" I asked.

"No. They don't get interviewed because they don't put in the extra effort. Most people don't have the balls to cross the *effort line* and take a gamble on giving all they've got in pursuing a position that isn't a sure thing. The ones who are successful at landing interviews and high-paying salaries are the ones who take risks and make direct contact with the employer. How else do you expect to get hired if you aren't willing to do whatever it takes to get noticed in this shattered economy?"

"Of course… that makes sense. But what happens if I can't find a name? It's so hard to figure out who to address it to when a lot of job postings I've seen so far do not include a contact name."

Emily paused for a moment and stood back. It looked like she was deep in thought, contemplating whether or not she should tell me what was on her mind.

"Listen," Emily said with hesitation. "I can give you something... a technique you could use, but you have to understand that what I'm about to tell you is classified," she warned. "If I reveal this to you, you cannot share this technique with anybody. Agreed?"

"Why? What's the big deal?"

"You're about to learn some inner-circle stuff, Adrian. The last thing either of us would want is to have this technique exposed all over the internet, making it overused and commonplace."

"Alright," I said, genuinely intrigued. "What is it?"

Emily rested her elbow on the table and leaned in closer to me. "Alright, here it is." She took another deep breath and continued. "Sometimes you just can't find the name of the hiring authority. That's a cold reality that many job seekers have had to come to terms with for the longest time. If that ever happens, here's what you do..." Emily pulled out her cell phone and dangled it in the air. I stared at it, wondering what she could mean.

I didn't want to seem dumb, like I had no idea what she was talking about, but I couldn't figure out what she was alluding to by putting her cell phone in my face. "What are you trying to say?" I asked.

"I'm sure it never dawned on you, but if you can't find out who to address your cover letter to, all you have to do is call the office."

"What do you mean, *call the office*?"

"You call them and say, 'Hi, I'm Adrian Addler. I'm writing a letter to the head of your 'whatever' department. Can I have the spelling of that person's name?' Odds are the employee at the front desk will give you the info and never think twice about it."

I scratched my chin. I had never heard of a line like that before. I was pretty impressed. "That's a crazy idea," I said. "Crazy—but good."

"It may be a little edgy for your taste," she laughed, "but when it comes to getting the job you want, you have to go out of your way to take the steps that will put you above the competition. Doing this will often mean doing things that you once thought were impossible... even crazy."

I liked the idea of separating myself from the pack, of having knowledge that few others possessed. Her words began to work on my imagination... "I see what you mean."

"No matter how you look at it, it certainly beats the alternative, which is to send a 'To Whom It May Concern' letter. Our society has programmed us to hate letters like that. It's the same as getting junk mail or a mass text message; all you want to do is scrap it or press DELETE."

"True," I agreed. I was beginning to see why Emily didn't want something like this to get out into the open; it would certainly ruin the 'WOW factor' if 500 people were dialing the company secretary and asking for names and addresses.

Emily continued with her lesson, putting the phone-call conversation aside for now.

"For some reason, people seem to think that an uninspiring, generic cover letter is professional. I don't know where this idea came from."

"Me neither..." I paused for a moment. I was still a little bit on the fence about putting in the extra effort, even though Emily had just explained everything so impressively. There was still something I couldn't quite put my finger on... something that was holding me back from taking the leap of faith and giving it my all in creating a cover letter.

"But do you really think it's *that* important to create a cover letter?"

"Lets put it this way: If you don't have a cover letter, the employer will think you're too lazy to write one or that you have poor writing skills and can't write one. Both will rule you out." She paused. "Remember to think of your cover letter as your own promotional team. The promotional team is working to make sure that a crowd shows up to your 'Main Event' (aka, your résumé).

"Most people won't want to go check out your show unless there's a promotional team talking up how cool it is inside. You gotta lure employers in by showing some personality in your cover letter. The *key* is creating a cover letter that does such a stand-up job promoting you that employers will *automatically* be dialing your digits to book an interview with you."

"OK... OK... I get it. I guess I can include one," I said, trying to pry her off my back. She looked at me and frowned. "And I'll make it *personal*. That shouldn't be too hard. But, beneath all this, it's not my cover letter I'm worried about." I lied. I was worried about everything.

"What's bothering you? Do you have doubts about your interviewing skills?" she asked.

"No, I feel like I've got pretty good interviewing skills (if I would ever get a damn callback). I just wish the whole hiring process wasn't based on a couple pieces of paper that they never teach you about in college."

"That's understandable," Emily said, "but are you comfortable with your interviewing skills?"

"Yeah, sure. I'm great with interviews."

"How many interviews have you been on?"

"Three," I said, clearing my throat. "But I'm naturally confident and well-spoken. People just seem to like me. My good interviewing skills were how I got my internship."

"I believe it," she said. "Interviewing is one of the most important, if not THE most important, obstacles when it comes to getting hired. An interview can make or break a candidate, regardless of virtually everything else."

"That's good news for me."

"Well... don't get too far ahead of yourself. As a recruiter, I work with people like you all the time, and I've learned a lot about what it means to be 'great with interviews,' and most people who *think* they're great are really just plain average. They just never see it because they've never physically seen themselves or others go through an entire interview."

"Well, I'm pretty sure I'm the exception to that rule. Like I said, if I could get more callbacks from employers, I don't think I would have any problems during the interview."

"Fair enough," Emily said. "But why aren't you getting the callbacks?"

"I just told you, the damn hiring process is flawed!" I was heated over this. It had been ruining my life for weeks, months, and no one else seemed to understand how screwed up everything really was.

"You don't think it has anything to do with you needing to improve your job-hunting skills?"

I paused. "Improve my job-hunting skills? What could I improve? There are only so many ways to push the 'send' button in your email!"

"That's not what I'm talking about. I'm talking about changing your overall *approach* to how you get interviews. Job hunting is a skill," she said. "It's like martial arts. You can't do all those fancy punches and ninja kicks until you build your skills, strengthen your core, and get your mind in the right place. You need to learn how to get the interview, how to get the employer interested in YOU instead of going in there blind and asking for a job.

"I think you need to change the way you present your résumé and cover letter. You need to change the way you research companies and how you present yourself in the interview."

"That sounds like a good idea, but I'm not really sure I know *how* to change it. I feel like I've been doing everything the best I can."

"From what I've seen, you've been doing it the way you've been taught. And really, that's not good enough to beat the masses."

"Well, I appreciate the help," I said.

"What do you mean? That's it? You don't want to work on your skills?"

"This is all a bit much for me," I said, standing up from the table and shuffling toward the staircase. I felt like I was in a maze of words and options. The echoes of her advice were swirling around me, dizzying me, making me nauseous and tired. "I just don't have the energy to work on this right now."

"Are you ever going to have the energy?"

"Maybe..." I began walking upstairs, feeling very overwhelmed. This whole *getting hired* thing had become something different than I'd imagined. Emily was part of a different school of thought, something elite. To be honest, I didn't know if I had the energy or the will power to meet her standards—to be a part of her circle of trust. I stopped on the staircase and told her this.

"You've got to do it, Adrian. This is not like you're trying out for high school basketball... Getting a job is going to determine the rest of your life." She stared at me, waiting for a response. "You're either in, or you're out. If you're in, we can talk again tomorrow and nail down some more-advanced techniques. If you're out, I won't bother you again."

I wondered about my chances of finding a job on my own. I could probably do it. But I'd turned in 40 applications so far without a single callback... With this economy it would be stupid to not take everything I could get. What did I have to lose by learning her secrets? What did I have to lose by being a bit more risky and aiming at a higher target?

"First of all, you're asking me to make some big changes. I appreciate what you're trying to do, but before I decide to tear up my cover letter and résumé I'm going to need a few hours to think about all of this."

I walked the rest of the way upstairs and sat down at my desk, pulling out my cover letter and résumé. I carried them across my bedroom, toward the far corner. I stood there silently, reading the first few lines of my cover letter as it dangled dangerously close to the trashcan.

"Alright, Adrian," I said to myself, "do you really want to do this?"

Part Two

"You didn't need to throw it in the trash," Emily laughed.

"I needed to get rid of it. I still have it saved on my computer, but there was something liberating about throwing it away. I even took the trash out afterward."

"You didn't recycle it? You're such a *green* kind of guy."

"Whatever. I forgot. But, I'm telling you right now that this doesn't mean you have full license to do whatever you want with my résumé. It means that I'm willing to hear your point of view on how to get hired."

"I appreciate your concessions," she mocked.

"So, Professor Anderson, where do we begin today?"

"Hmm... Let's see..." She twirled her finger in her hair. "Interviewing is all about *perception*. Every little thing that you do during your job hunt gives the employer a certain perception of you as a potential candidate: the way you format your résumé, the way you write the opening sentence in your cover letter, whether or not you've spent any time proofreading for typos. All of these little details are like brushstrokes that paint a bigger picture for the employers of the type of person you would be if they hired you. You just need to ask yourself, 'Am I painting myself to be more valuable than the average job applicant?' If you're not, you need to change your tactics."

A multitude of thoughts flooded into my head: Maybe I wasn't working hard enough? Maybe I needed to focus my energy in different areas? Maybe I needed to spend more time on my job search? I hated the idea of sacrificing my last sacred "college days" for my job hunt, but I knew I didn't have a choice.

Emily continued, "Think about it like this: There are three types of people who apply for jobs. The first type are those who are most qualified for the job but have terrible résumés and sub-par interviewing skills. These types of people are called the true *Under Dogs* of the job market, and they miss opportunities every day because of their sub-par presentation skills.

"The second type are what we call *Smooth Talkers*. They're really good at promoting themselves in a way that lands them almost any job they want. They have a natural ability to market themselves. Although, most, if not all, of these types of people are notorious for underperforming in their jobs. They are masters of 'gaming the system' once they're hired.

"The third type are those who are both really good at promoting themselves while also being the most qualified for the job. These types of people are called *Stars*. Needless to say, this is where you want to aim. I feel like you, Adrian, are among the *Under Dogs*. You're fully qualified but need to improve your job-hunting skills. You've told me time and again that you're a very hard worker and that your supervisors compliment you all the time."

"I am a good worker," I said.

"I know you are. The problem is that you're not demonstrating this on your résumé, and therefore you're not getting called back."

"You think so?"

"Yeah, I do. And here's a good example that will illustrate exactly what I'm talking about:

"Before I graduated I knew this guy who was kind of an introvert. You see, to me, he was a 'let's just be friends' kind of guy. He wasn't particularly charming, didn't dress very well, and looked like a scrub. I really didn't think any girl would ever be interested in him. He was a great friend, but he wasn't very sexually attractive. Anyway, I think there was literally only one girl on campus that liked him, and she was in my poli-sci class. She would hound me every day asking me all these questions about him. One day I just couldn't take it anymore and I asked her, 'Why are you so into Jason?'"

"And what did she say?" I probed.

"Apparently, they had gotten wasted at a party once and slept together, and she said he was, you know, good in bed."

"Good for Jason..." I said, shrugging my shoulders to elude the fact that I was missing the relevance of the story.

"Just let me finish," she defended, shaking her head and gathering her thoughts. "The funny thing is I asked Jason how his dating life was, and he told me that other than the one girl, no other girls were interested in him."

"That sucks."

"Exactly. He was a great lay, but he had a hard time *getting* laid."

"Like I said, that sucks."

"OK, and let me tell you about a time I experienced the exact *opposite*. About three years ago, just before I got with Josh, I was on a spree of failed dating attempts. I had gone out with three or four guys in a short period of time, and none of them were up to my standards. Finally I met a guy who was smart, charming, and good-looking... someone girls always seemed to gravitate toward."

"OK..." I said, not understanding exactly where this was going.

"So, we went on a few dates and I kept thinking, 'This guy is so smooth!' He really seemed like he could be the perfect match for me."

"And what happened?"

"Well, when it came time to sleep with him, he was just... bad in bed."

"What do you mean?"

"He just had no idea how to turn a woman on. It felt like he was trying to puncture my lungs rather than give me an orgasm..." She raised her eyebrows. "And beforehand he spent about three minutes sticking his tongue in my ear." She covered her face with her hands, trying to block the images from her head. She spoke through her palms, "It was literally like getting hit on the side of the head with a big wave... Or a large... wet... *jellyfish*—"

"Gross!" I said, cutting her off. "That's enough."

"Yeah, you're right... Let's just say he turned me off and I didn't want to have anything to do with him. I slept with him *once*, and that was that."

I was still a little confused as to why Emily had decided to divulge so much about her sexual past with me and so I asked, "How does this relate to me getting a job?"

"Don't you see what I'm saying? Sometimes getting a job is exactly like having a tongue in your ear," she joked.

"Ha! Ha!" I bellowed sarcastically.

"No, but seriously, getting a job is the same as getting laid. Some people have sex all the time because of their charisma and presentation skills, even though they're terrible in bed. Other people are the exact opposite: They are really good in bed but have no charm and poor presentation skills; therefore, they never get laid."

"So having sex is like getting the job?"

"That's right. Remember this: There's no relationship between being good and getting hired."

"That is the most bizarre analogy I've ever heard... but, strangely enough, I see what you mean. So you're basically saying that I'm like Jason: I can perform on the job, but all the stuff before that isn't so great."

"Like the way you present your résumé and cover letter."

"At least I'm good in bed," I joked.

"That's great, but being good in bed isn't worth anything if you can't find someone to sleep with."

"Yeah, I see what you mean. But wait, what about the last group? Someone who is both charming and good in bed?"

"I'd tell you about that, but Josh doesn't like it when I discuss our sex life in public," she said with a smile.

I shook my head.

Emily's cell phone rang. She darted up the staircase and answered. I walked into the living room, my laptop in hand, and began doing some research on Empyrean. Emily had told me several weeks ago to make an account on LinkedIn.com, so I took a few minutes to do that. LinkedIn was a good way to research the companies I was applying for and to see what type of people worked for them. I typed "Empyrean" into the search bar. I clicked through the results. Almost the entire Board of Directors was there—the CEO, VP, high-ranking sales reps, basically everyone who worked for the company.

"Alright, Adrian," Emily called. "I gotta run. Do me, and yourself, a favor: Make a list of the top 20 companies you want to work for."

"Twenty? That seems like a lot."

"Yeah, well, you'll need plenty of companies to practice with before you gun for Empyrean. And don't forget, not every company you apply to is going to call you in for an interview. Just make sure Empyrean is the last name on the list. That way we have a pecking order that we can go off of when you actually start submitting résumés. Oh, and spend some time researching Empyrean, and maybe tonight or tomorrow we can work on making changes to your résumé."

"Yeah, I will," I said. "Have fun at Josh's thing."

"I will!"

And she was gone. After an hour or so I went on a walk and stopped by Jake's house for lunch. I'd left a loaf of bread and some sandwich meat in his fridge. I reached in and helped myself.

"What are you getting into today?" he asked.

"Nothing. I've been trying to figure out how I'm going to apply to Empyrean."

"Empyrean? I remember you talking about them junior year, but I didn't think anything would ever come of it."

"I've been doing the research, getting myself ready for the challenge."

"You're not kidding around, huh?"

"Well, at the rate I'm going it will be a miracle if *anyone* hires me. Did I tell you that I've applied to 40 companies? Guess how many I've heard back from?"

"How many?"

"Zero."

"Whoa," he said, cocking his head in disbelief. "*None* of those companies called you back?"

"Nope."

"I don't get it, man. You have such a good track record. It sucks that you can't find a job."

"It's the damn economy…"

"Yeah, but you're not some deadbeat. A guy like you, a guy who has his head on straight and his shit together, shouldn't have this much trouble getting a job."

"I wish it was that way," I said dismally. "Anyway, no sense in pissing and moaning about it. I've been doing research to get ready for Empyrean. I really want to work there, and if I'm going to compete with the other résumés I've got to be as prepared as possible."

I ate the rest of my lunch and went down to the school library. It was 2:00 p.m. and I somehow managed to research Empyrean until the evening hours. I went for a long walk around campus and stopped by the gym to shoot hoops. After an hour of basketball I walked home and fell asleep on the couch. I hadn't done much that day, but I was mentally exhausted from the hours and hours of reading on the computer.

Something startled me from sleep and I reached out toward a fuzzy blue light. It was my cell phone. Isabelle had sent me a text message. I opened it:

I'm at a party on Grace St.
Wanna hang out?

PART THREE

I woke up at 7:00 a.m. the following morning and walked downstairs. Emily was already awake.

"I take it you didn't find anything to do last night?" Emily asked.

"No," I said, remembering Isabelle's text with mixed feelings. "It just didn't seem like much was going on."

"Yeah. That's the way it is some nights."

I sat down at the table and poured a glass of water. I was starting to feel a bit like a homebody. But what was I supposed to do? My bank account was overdrafted and I had no money coming in. I couldn't go to parties or bars or play golf… I couldn't really do ANYTHING except look for another job, a task I had so far been a colossal failure at completing.

"You make your list?" Emily asked.

"Yeah. I found about 15 companies that I wouldn't mind working for. I can only really see myself working for about four of them. Empyrean is still my first choice."

"Did you do the research on Empyrean?"

"Yeah," I said casually. "About eight hours' worth."

"You really like that company, don't you?"

"You could say that."

"So, what sort of research did you get done?"

"I made a profile on LinkedIn like you told me to, and I searched the job listings there and researched the Empyrean execs."

"Cool, cool… Did you look anywhere else for job listings?"

"Yeah. I checked Craigslist.org, Monster.com, Careerbuilder.com, and… umm… Simplyhired.com. I think that's it."

"Good. Sounds like you hit most of them." Emily stretched her arms into the air and yawned. She stood up and paced the kitchen, looking for something. "Now, Adrian, you know you can't keep sending out that same old résumé…"

"What do you mean?"

"Here it is," she reached into a pile of paperwork and pulled out my résumé. "This thing looks… well… it looks like a rusty old pickup truck."

"Take it easy," I said, snatching the résumé from her. "This is exactly how I was taught in school. My professor was a doctorate of... something important."

"Well, your professor did what he thought was best. He taught you how to drive a rusty pickup truck into a parking lot full of rusty pickup trucks and beg for a paint job."

"This thing looks pretty good to me," I said. "In all honesty, I don't think it needs a whole lot of work."

"Adrian..." she looked up at me and raised her eyebrows.

"What?" I shrugged my shoulders, claiming innocence. "It's not *that* bad!"

She looked back at the résumé. "It's pretty bad. The problem is that it looks *exactly* like everyone else's, and everyone else's look like... I don't know... *obituaries!*"

I couldn't believe her analogies. First it was rusty pickup trucks, now it was dead people... where would it end? I read over the résumé again.

"It looks alright to me."

"Seriously?"

"Yeah, seriously. Look at this thing!" I said, bringing a tone of confidence to my voice. "The margins are perfect, the font sizes are cool, and I've got a cool border—*that's* something that I made different. See?" I pointed to my border. "I came up with that myself. Oh, and I totally forgot to mention the font. It's called Silian Rail." I smiled proudly, explaining to Emily that Jake had searched the internet and found the font specifically for my résumé.

"OK, enough about the résumé. Let's put that aside and come back to it later... Tell me more about Empyrean. Did you find out a list of their competitors?"

"I went to a website called Hoovers.com, which had almost everything I needed to know. It showed me all of Empyrean's locations, gave me an overview of the company's performance, provided me with Empyrean press releases, and also listed their competition."

"Not bad," Emily said.

"Empyrean's major competitor is Proteus & Paulson, who also had some job postings on LinkedIn. They are on my top-15 list. I looked up some of Proteus & Paulson's employees' profiles just to get a feel for who they were hiring."

"Sounds like you put in some long hours."

"Not as long as I thought. I estimated it would be a three-day job, but it didn't take that long once I got started."

"Good," Emily said quickly. "Do you have the names of some of the P&P employees on your computer?"

"Yeah," I pulled up a short list. "Not everybody was listed on LinkedIn. I kind of had a hard time finding them."

"Yeah, LinkedIn is somewhat new for many companies. They're probably just catching wind of its existence. Sometimes, if LinkedIn doesn't work, you have to search the internet in other places. Just be creative, that's one of the keys to being successful at this stuff." She paused, reading over my list of names. "Here we go," she pointed to a name. "John Mercer, Internet Administrator at Proteus & Paulson… he looks like the highest rank that you found. It sucks that he's not in the department you're applying for, but he's the best thing you've got. You'll use him to pony up the name of who you *really* need to speak with."

"Wait… so do I write my cover letter to him?"

"Well, no. He's the one we're going to call to find out about the company, and to find out who you need to talk to about getting hired."

I actually laughed out loud. "I don't know what they taught you at your recruiting job, but calling P&P and talking to an IT guy is totally out of the question. What if I mess up? It would ruin my chances of getting the job!"

"You didn't give me a chance to explain. *You* don't call the IT guy. What was his name?" She looked at the computer. "You don't call John Mercer."

"What are you talking about?" I felt like I was getting in over my head. This stuff sounded too risky, too impossible, too "mad scientist," if you will. I didn't have the time or energy to be fooling around with weird techniques. I needed to get hired; I didn't need to waste time making weird phone calls to IT people.

"I don't know if I want to do this," I told her. "I trust you and everything, but I have no idea what you're talking about. One minute you're telling me to call someone, the next minute you're telling me I shouldn't… I just don't understand what you want me to do."

"If you'll just be patient, I'm trying to let you in on a technique that I learned a while back," she said.

"I don't know if I'm up for any more 'secret' techniques…"

"OK, I see... so you want to keep beating your head against the wall and missing out on even more job offers? You're fine with settling for less than what you're worth?"

"That's not what I'm saying. I just don't know about all of this..."

"Adrian, what is there not to know? You've applied for 40 jobs and haven't heard a WORD from anybody! It's about time you took some action and made a move on these people. I'm trying to give you some field-tested advice... some *proven* strategies that employers do not want you to know."

"I know, you explained that already... *no employers want 500 people calling their company, etc., etc.*"

"Enough with the sarcasm. You want the job at Empyrean, right?"

"Yeah."

"And you want to hone your skills by applying to P&P, right?"

"Yeah."

"And you KNOW that I'm a professional, that I'm good at this stuff, and that I've given a dozen of my friends this information and they've ALL used it to get better jobs."

I was getting frustrated. Emily made me feel like I didn't know what I was doing. I almost wanted to tell her to stop, to leave me on my own, that all this new information was too much, but she had piqued my interest with her last remark.

"Wait a second... So, you're telling me that a dozen people got a job based on this ONE tactic you're about to teach me?"

"Not this tactic alone, but this is what opened the doors for them to get an interview."

"OK... so what is it? Who calls this guy..." I looked at the screen and read his name. "John Mercer. Who calls John Mercer, and what the hell do they say when they get him on the line?"

"Think of it like this: It's like in *Ferris Bueller's Day Off* when Ferris gets his buddy to call the school and say that Ferris is sick. It's the same idea. You have one of your friends call P&P and say, 'Hello, this is John Smith, may I please speak with John Mercer?' You follow me?"

"Maybe... I don't know if I like it..."

She scoffed. "You've got to step outside of that rusty old pickup truck. You've got to get out of your comfort zone and separate yourself from the pack. I can teach you all sorts of tricks that I've learned from my own job hunts and from watching literally hundreds, if not thousands, of people's successes and failures, but if you're not willing to act on my advice, I'm wasting my breath."

"Well, I guess I don't really have anything to lose. If all this fails I'll just go back to school and get my MBA. That might be a good idea anyway. Then I'll make even more money once I graduate."

"Oh, please... stop running back to your safety blanket." Emily put her hands up, stopping herself from going further. "Sorry if that was a bit mean, but I've heard the same song so many times from college students: 'If I just get my MBA...' Like that's some sort of magic ticket! An MBA is just going to lose you money in the long run. Think of all the wages you'll lose, the experience you'll miss out on. While everyone else is out there MAKING money, you'll be SPENDING it on more school."

"I never thought of it that way."

"Let's not think about that stuff right now. You need to get the job at Empyrean, and to get that job you need to practice on some of Empyrean's competitors to see exactly how the game is played in their industry."

"So..." I said, entertaining her wild ideas. "Somebody calls this IT guy... What's the reason for the call? Like I said, *I'm* not going to make any phone calls to someone at P&P. That would be like committing career suicide before you ever have a career."

Emily laughed.

"What's so funny?"

"You said it would be like committing career suicide." She was still giggling a bit.

"Yeah, it would be. If I called P&P and tried to speak to some guy I didn't even know, odds are they'd write me off as a nut job. Why are you laughing?"

"Because it's funny that you likened it to suicide."

"Why's that funny?" I was beginning to think Emily might be losing it.

"Because, the technique is called Suicide Calling. The beauty is that *you* don't call them; *I* do. And therefore, you do not commit career suicide. Suicide Calling is an art. I've had lots of success with it, and you will too. Just trust me." She patted me on the arm. "Let me make a phone call to this John Mercer guy. You'll thank me in the long run."

"You're sure this stuff really works?"

"It's how I got my job at Harrell-Finch."

"OK, OK… so it's a tried-and-true tactic. I get that. Now tell me a bit about how it works. What will you say to him?"

"I'll call the front desk and ask for John Mercer. I'll stay on the line for an hour if it takes that long. I'll get connected to Mercer and move around from there. Maybe he'll transfer me to someone else. Maybe he'll want to chat and answer my questions. People LOVE spitting off information. You'd be surprised how many people are bored in their jobs and welcome a conversation from a person they don't even know."

"Are you serious? You've ACTUALLY done this before?"

"Probably 50 times."

"Holy shit… that's nuts."

"Suicide Calling is crazy. The beauty is that we have nothing to lose. I don't want to work for P&P, so it doesn't matter if I cross the line when I'm asking questions. And, believe me, the longer I can stay on the line, the deeper I will probe, until I know what kind of personality they're looking to hire, for what projects they need people, how many they need. I'll also find out how their company is doing financially (something most interviewees are afraid of asking on a first phone call), what things are like on a day-to-day basis… maybe I'll even be able to climb the chain of command until someone transfers me to the president of the company!" She laughed excitedly, getting a bit carried away. She really got into this type of stuff. "I'll make them sick and tired of hearing my voice. I'll do literally ANYTHING to find out EXACTLY who they're looking for and how YOU can fit the bill."

"OK," I said, a bit overwhelmed. I needed to see this thing in action in order to understand it. "I'm going to let you handle this. Take it away."

"And remember, we'll treat this P&P experiment as if you're applying for a job with Empyrean. We'll work up to Empyrean, but if you happen to get another job along the way, it won't hurt to have two companies vying for your services. This is the only way you'll have a rebound plan. And rebound plans are good, because they get you out of the 'scarcity mindset,' which is a dangerous place to be."

"If anyone's ever had a scarcity mindset, it's me. I'm 0 for 40 on the job hunt. I need a miracle."

She smiled, patting me on the back. "We'll figure this out together," she said. "Don't worry. I'm not giving up until you're behind a desk at Empyrean making your dreams come true."

"Touching," I said sarcastically.

Two minutes later I was sitting beside her, the phone on speaker, and she was skillfully dodging around P&P's receptionist.

PART FOUR

"Hi, this is Emily Anderson calling for John Mercer please."

"Let me see…" The woman checked on something. "Just one moment please."

I was amazed that Emily had gotten through. She sounded so casual yet so direct that the woman had assumed it was an important phone call from someone he knew.

"John Mercer," the man said.

"Hi, my name's Emily Anderson, I'm a student at the university. I heard you are hiring for an associate position?"

I scrambled to find a pen and pad of paper to take notes on. I couldn't believe she actually got through to him. I had to remember *everything* this guy said on the phone.

"Several," Mr. Mercer said. He was preoccupied and Emily struggled to engage him.

"So… what type of person is the company interested in hiring?"

"Well, I'm not sure I can accurately answer a question like that. I work in the IT department. You're going to want to talk to HR for that. Let me forward you…"

Emily abruptly cut him off, "Wait! Before you do that… If you don't mind me asking a quick question: How did you know you were hiring several junior associates if you work in IT?" It was obvious she was trying to avoid the black hole otherwise known as HR. I had similar experiences in some of my earlier phone-call attempt to call a company; they would transfer me to HR and I would be forwarded directly to their automated voice-message system.

"Because I manage the database for all the job postings in the company."

"Oh, OK… that makes sense. You know, you just reminded me of something else that I've always been curious about with the tech industry. Has the economy affected your department at all in terms of workload?"

Mercer sat in silence for a moment then replied, "It hasn't affected us in terms of workload. Technology pretty much runs itself, so there really isn't any difference in the amount of work that needs to be done. Job security, on the other hand, has definitely been affected by the economy. I know a few people who used to work for IT departments in other companies that have already been let go. When the economy goes south, IT is usually one of the first departments to experience cutbacks."

"Really? I had no idea..."

"Yeah, its really rough out there. I've heard of entire families with no money to feed their children or pay off their mortgages."

"Wow... that's really a shame." Emily was really trying hard to empathize with Mercer and make a connection.

"I guess I made an amateur assumption that since more people were getting laid off there would be more people applying for positions, which I thought would mean more work for the people managing the websites..." Emily was searching for a piece of information. I had a feeling she was about to get it.

"No, not really. Like I said, all of our systems are pretty much automated. Whenever a job applicant applies for a position through our website it automatically gets stored into our database. Our rigorous scanning software goes through and filters through all the major keywords, pulling up only those résumés that match the specific criteria that we're looking for."

"Well, that sounds a heck of a lot easier than how I thought it was done. I thought there was a whole team of people reading those things."

"Nah... the hiring team only reads the applications that make it through our scanning software. Right now, they've got... hmmm..." He typed something on his keyboard and Emily nodded excitedly and pointed at the phone. "We've got just under 400 applications," he said.

"Wow, 400 applications! Was that before or after the scanning software was done with it?"

"After."

I shook my head in disbelief, writing the number on my piece of paper.

"So, is there an executive leader for the hiring team? Someone in charge of making the final decisions for who does or doesn't make the cut? Would that be you?" she said with a smile. Emily's tone was on the verge of flirtatious.

The man chuckled, "That's not me, but yeah, there's someone that should take care of stuff like that." He remained quiet, obviously distracted by something else. Emily tapped her nails on the kitchen table.

"Well, is there any way you could help me get connected with them? I'd really appreciate anything you could do for me."

"Umm… I don't know…"

"Please…" Emily said.

"Look, I'm not supposed to do this, but you need to talk to Ken Barnes. He just walked out a few minutes ago. I heard him say he'd be back in an hour."

"Thanks," Emily said. "Is there a number where he can be reached?"

"That's as much as I can tell you. I'm really not supposed to give out his information, much less his desk number…" Mr. Mercer said.

"If Mr. Barnes would be the fastest and most direct way for me to have my questions answered, I would greatly appreciate *anything* you could do to put me in touch with him," Emily said. She was capable of pressing Mercer, even to the point where a potential applicant would have been slightly out of line. After all, she wasn't really applying for the job. She had a license to say and do whatever she wanted.

Finally, after several more minutes of question and answer, Mr. Mercer agreed to give Emily the number. She winked at me as she read the number into the speaker phone for confirmation. I actually stood up.

The phone call ended, and we slapped hands. It had worked excellently. Now, either Emily or I could make the phone call to Ken Barnes. It was like finding Wonka's Golden Ticket.

"That was awesome," I said.

"Well, we're not quite done."

"What do you mean?"

"I'm going to call Mr. Barnes myself. Then we'll draft the résumé. And trust me, your résumé will be SOLID after we redo it. It will be a good trial run before we hit Empyrean."

"So, you really want me to redo my whole résumé?" I asked.

"I'm going to be honest, Adrian: Your résumé looks like shit. I've told you this ten times already." She picked it up from across the table and shook her head. "I know a lot about… well…" she paused. "How can I explain this?" she asked.

"Don't ask me," I joked. "I have no idea what you're talking about."

"There are techniques I've learned from my job as a recruiter. I've figured out all these little ways you can get your résumé noticed. I mean, in all seriousness, haven't you ever realized that every single résumé and cover letter looks pretty much the same? Even the 'good' ones?"

"I know, I know... rusty pickup trucks. I've heard this lecture already this morning. 'They're all rusty pickup trucks, a whole parking lot full of them, and I'm just sitting alongside the masses.'"

"Now you're catching on!" she joked. "Trust me, this won't be nearly as painful as you're making it out to be. I know some really simple ways to make your résumé stand out and become more impressive. Suicide Calling is just the beginning. There's a whole secret method to making your résumé irresistible to employers. You'll give each employer EXACTLY what they're looking for."

"Sounds good to me," I said. "At this point I guess I'm up for trying anything."

"I'll show you more stuff later. I've got to go meet Josh right now. We're taking down the art from his gallery show last night. I'll call Mr. Barnes when I get back."

"I'll be here," I said.

"Oh yeah, Adrian, do some research on Ken Barnes. See if you can find an article from a newspaper or something, anything... maybe an interview he did. You need to find something that is published about him before we make the call."

"How do you suppose I do that?" I asked. "I have no idea where to even begin looking."

"You'll be fine. Just search his name under Google News or something. Dig around a bit; you'll find it. I believe in you."

"Alright..." I said, typing his name into the search engine. "Whatever you say."

*   *   *

Lunch hour passed and I worked on my résumé nonstop, trying to make it so good that Emily would have no room to complain.

An hour later Emily came through the front door, smiling and ending a conversation on her cell phone about Terrier puppies or something... Emily didn't have a care in the world. Her constant good moods made me envy her general success in life.

"You look up some info on Barnes?" she asked.

"Yeah, I found this interview he did in the *Tribune*."

"Great... this works," she said, reading over the printout. "Good... good... yeah, I can use this."

"What are you using it for?"

"You'll see in a minute. Let's do this thing,"

Josh, Emily's boyfriend, stood back and laughed. It was amazing to him how quick-witted she was. He must have loved to watch her work, to see her secret methods in action. No one could figure out how she was so successful, how she knew so much. It was just the way she was. I began to think that maybe there was a way I could learn to be that way as well...

We dialed the number, and I rolled the pen between my fingers.

"Proteus & Paulson," the receptionist answered. "This is Ann speaking."

"Hi, Ann, this is Emily Andersen. I'm calling for Ken Barnes."

"May I ask what this is regarding?"

"Well, I know this may sound a bit odd, but I'm a business student at the university and just read his interview in the *Tribune*. I have been following his career for quite some time now and have finally built up the courage to call him for one specific piece of advice. It would take no more than two minutes of his time, and I promise I won't waste a minute of it. Is there any way you can help me get through to him?"

"Alright, I'll check his availability... let me see."

Several moments passed in silence. Emily stared pensively at the telephone. "Here you go, Ms. Andersen."

The conversation began, Emily talking a mile a minute and Ken Barnes responding just as quickly. Within 10 minutes, Emily had figured out the type of person Mr. Barnes intended to hire.

"I need a guy who likes to solve problems and who likes working with a team. Experience working with a team is good, but experience in this field isn't going to make or break the deal for me. We have a good training program here at P&P."

I wrote it down. I remembered last summer solving problems as an intern while working in a team environment. I was starting to see how this information could work for me.

After 10 or 15 minutes, much longer than anyone could have guessed, Mr. Barnes had to abruptly end the conversation to jump into another phone meeting.

"Satisfied?" Emily asked.

"Hell yeah," I said. "That was awesome. How did you know what to ask? Anyone could have called up there like that, but where did you come up with all those questions? I've never heard anybody ask things like that when they're trying to get a job."

"It's all part of Suicide Calling. There's a definite science behind it. You need to remember how I did it in order to succeed. Did you write down the list of questions and answers?"

"Yeah, I did," I said. During the whole conversation I had been busy taking down names, notes, and any other nuances I thought could be instrumental in getting the job.

I could also tell from the Suicide Calling experiment that Emily was much more experienced than I was. Her verbal skills made me realize that my interviewing tactics needed work—and by interviewing I mean more than the face-to-face interaction with an employer. Interviewing skills include imperative front-end research, crafting a good-looking résumé and cover letter, and making yourself stand out so that you will be noticed through a sea of potential hires.

"This has been really awesome," I said.

"Yeah, it has. There's no better way to get a job."

"I believe it," I said.

"But remember, there's so much more to learn."

"I can imagine," I said. "I feel like I've learned so much already, but I can sense that this is merely the tip of the iceberg."

"It's the *very* tip," she said. "Suicide Calling, making a great résumé, all of the skills you need to get a job, don't come easy for most people. Honestly, we haven't really gone into a fraction of the detail that we need to on each of these skills. But, that will come with time."

"I'm willing to put in the time," I said. "I'm starting to get kind of excited about this."

"You have to be more than excited. You've got to *want* a job more than you've ever wanted anything in your whole life. Literally."

I nodded my head. "I do. I also wanted to say that I appreciate you helping me with all of this."

"Sure, I've got no problem helping as long as you're willing to *take action* on the methods that I teach. Understanding the secrets to getting hired is easy, but simply getting it on an intellectual level isn't enough. You need to physically change your behavior and *take action*. It's quite a challenge to be the best, and many people sink before they've even left the dock."

"I believe it…"

Emily had shown me her secret world, and now I was navigating a labyrinth of behavioral code, deciphering the methods necessary to create a bond between the employer and myself. I suddenly realized that there was more behind the interviewing process than I had originally thought.

In fact, successful interviewing had a great deal to do with understanding human nature. There was an intricate matrix of physical, emotional, and intellectual obstacles that lay ahead of me in what seemed like an incredibly complicated and impenetrable hiring process.

I could tell that I was barely scratching the surface with what needed to be learned. And, what's more, I knew I couldn't do it on my own. Getting through Suicide Calling was only the beginning of the challenges that lay ahead of me. I had yet to meet the faces behind these companies and watch them in the field. I would soon find out who they were, and more importantly, what made them tick.

And so began the strangest four months of my life…

THE FIRST PROBLEM FOR
ALL OF US, MEN AND
WOMEN, IS NOT TO LEARN,
BUT TO UNLEARN.

••••••••••••••••••••••••••••

–GLORIA STEINEM,
American Writer and Activist

CHAPTER 2

INITIATION

Seventy students were cramped in the lecture hall. Professor Hackmuth, our beloved economics "guru," was running his mouth as usual. I hadn't been paying attention for the past half hour. Nobody had. It was virtually impossible to make it past the 10-minute mark in that class without losing sanity. If you tried to stay on the same page, you'd have a mental collapse.

Jake, who always sat behind me in Hackmuth's class, tapped my shoulder. I waved him off and shook my head. I knew what he wanted to do…

"I say we bail," he whispered.

"He's only got 10 more minutes," I said.

"Yeah, but that's 10 minutes I can spend somewhere else. Life's too short for this," he laughed.

I began to gather my things and thought against it. "Just wait a minute. I can't take off yet. This guy's gunning for me. If I leave class early he might lower my participation grade. I don't want to get a 'C' for this quarter."

Professor Hackmuth looked in our direction and pursed his lips. He continued speaking. His words didn't make sense. I tried to listen, but it sounded like he wasn't even speaking English. I didn't understand… I couldn't make sense of a single sentence. I shook my head and pretended to take notes.

My attention perked when Hackmuth explained that he was passing back the quizzes from last week. He walked up the aisles and handed the papers face down to each student, nodding at those who had done well. He handed me my paper, nodded ever so slightly, and continued down the row. I flipped over my quiz and peeked at the grade.

"Well done, Mr. Calloway," I heard Hackmuth say.

I quickly looked to my right, five seats down, where the self-proclaimed "genius" Kyle Calloway sat. Kyle's family owned CommuniTea, a multi-billion-dollar tea company that had originally been a part of the East India Trading Company. He had more money than some small countries and chose to flaunt it whenever possible.

The girl sitting next to Kyle congratulated him, pulling playfully at his shirt sleeve. He smiled and straightened his collar from where she had misaligned it.

I stood up to leave and walked down the stairs. As I was exiting the lecture hall, I felt a tap on my right shoulder.

"Adrian?"

I turned around and stared blankly at the young woman. I had seen her before, but had no recollection of her name. "Yes?" I asked.

"Aren't you in business finance with Professor Bryant?"

"Yeah, I am."

"We have that group project due and I was wondering if you wanted to join a group that I've formed."

"Yeah, sure, that would be great," I said.

"Business finance is such an awesome course."

I shrugged. "Yeah, I guess it is."

"It makes this class seem *so* boring."

"I think there's more to it than just that…" I glanced at Hackmuth.

"I know what you mean," she said, widening her eyes to exaggerate her impatience with Hackmuth's lectures. "Speaking of him, how did you do on the quiz?"

"I got an 84%. How did you do…" I let my words hang, indicating that I couldn't remember her name.

"It's Lacy. Lacy Ashford."

"Right, I knew that…"

"I did OK on the test—87%."

"I don't think either of us did as well as Kyle Calloway." I watched him from the door as he spoke to Hackmuth. They were smiling, obviously going over answers from the test.

"Well, I don't think many people *could* do as well as Kyle without, you know…" She rolled her eyes at the wall.

"What do you mean?"

"The whole time we were taking the test, Kyle had his cell phone on his lap. I got up to ask Hackmuth a question and saw that he had the answers typed into his iPhone."

"No shit..." I said, smiling in disbelief. "He's such a smart guy, why the hell's he need to do that?"

"Couldn't tell you," she said. "All I know is that he was doing it. I guess he's just trying to be a good role model for the rest of us... after all, he is the International Business Club president."

"Well..." I said, unable to come up with a response. Honestly, I didn't know the guy. I had heard good things, bad things, but had never passed judgment. Beneath it all, I had always thought there was something shady about him.

"I have to run. I'll see you in finance," Lacy said.

"Sure," I nodded. She darted through the door, and I walked slowly behind her, contemplating Calloway's cell-phone-cheating operation.

I went across the quad and made conversation with a couple of old friends. The talk was brief, and I was soon walking through the parking lot. For some reason, I couldn't remember where I had parked. The entire lot looked exactly the same and as I paced the rows I walked slowly, watching the birds chase one another between the trees.

"Hey, Addler!"

I looked down from the sky at a black BMW M6. The top was gone and sitting in the driver's seat was none other than Kyle Calloway. Who else would be driving a $108,000 car around campus?

"How's it going, Kyle?" I asked, hardly slowing my pace as he rolled along beside me.

"It's going alright," he said, the usual pretty-boy grin smearing itself across his face. "How you doin', bud?"

Bud? Why did he call me *bud*? I hardly knew him. "I'm doing alright. Glad to be out of class for the day."

"I hear that," he said. "How did you do on the Hackmuth thing?" He pointed toward the lecture hall.

"I did alright." I shrugged my shoulders, indicating that it was none of his business anyhow.

He cocked his head sideways, "Come on man, I was just *asking*. I always like to know what *Adrian Addler* got on a test. We're on the same team, you and me!" He pointed back and forth between us.

Same team my ass. Why was this guy sucking up to me? Kyle Calloway, from what I had seen, was an entirely different person when he was around guys like me. He tried to come off as a "buddy," but this behavior was merely a front for some un-nameable ulterior motive.

"Yeah, Kyle... same team," I agreed.

"That's what I like to hear," he said.

Kyle Calloway... what a piece of work. Kyle was the type of guy that everyone thinks is cool and is always the social center of the room. But, when he was around girls, which I had seen several times at the bar, he would try to gain their attention by being overly confident and masculine.

The scary thing was that when he put on this mask, I could see how normal, non-gold-digging girls could actually be attracted to him.

"Adrian, buddy," he said, "you're the standard by which I judge my success in school."

"Give me a break," I laughed. "If it really means that much to you, I got an 84%."

I felt obligated to ask him how he had fared, which was exactly what he wanted. Kyle hadn't asked me to find out what I got, he had asked me so that I would ask him what *he* got.

"I did alright, I guess... 96%."

"Not bad," I repeated, thinking all the while about his cheating scam.

Kyle's cell phone rang and he answered, holding a finger up to me as though he still wanted to talk.

"Hey, babe," he said into the phone. "How's Cali?" It must have been his girlfriend. "Really? That's great. I'm glad you guys are having a good time. Make sure you *learn* something at that conference!" he laughed exaggeratedly. "Alright, well, I'm on the road, just give me a call tomorrow at lunch... OK... talk to you later. Love you too."

He ended the call and slowed the car to a halt. I felt obligated to stop walking.

"So man..." his tone became more serious. "I heard through the grapevine that they're not keeping you at the internship. I wanted to tell you that I'm sorry, and that I feel your pain."

"Yeah..." I said. "It's nothing personal. Budgetary cutbacks. I'll be fine. In fact, I'm kind of excited about looking for something somewhere else."

"That's my kinda thinker," he said. He talked to me like a damn peewee hockey coach.

"Alright, well, I gotta—" A beautiful girl, probably a sophomore, cut me off in the middle of my sentence by hopping the door of Kyle's convertible and sliding into the front seat.

"Damn it," Kyle yelled, "you know I *hate* it when you do that! What if you kicked the dashboard or…"

"Relax," she said. "What is all this *junk*?" She pinched his Crew Team bag with two fingers, grimacing at the smell of man-sweat, and flung it into the back seat. There was also a stack of envelopes, which she set on his lap. I don't know why, but I was still standing there. I felt uncompelled to walk away. This was far too interesting.

"This is my *shit*," Kyle said. "You don't move *my* shit." He set the envelopes in the back seat, shoving them beneath his crew bag. A giant "C" was embroidered on the side of his bag. It was sewn there as a reminder to everyone else that Kyle Calloway was the *Captain* of the Crew Team, an accomplishment almost unimaginable at a university as competitive as ours.

I noticed that Kyle had kept one envelope in his lap. He looked up and handed it to me. "Check it out."

I took the envelope, opened it, and read. It was a letter from Pacific Crest accepting him for employment.

"Congratulations," I said. "That's great news."

"Not exactly," he smiled. "I told them no."

"Really?"

"Yeah, really. Pacific Crest isn't the company they used to be. Or, at least, people have hyped them up too much. The offer sucked. I told them to shove it up their asses."

"Wow," I said, reading the letter and passing it back to him.

"Kyle, let's roll… I have to get back to my sorority before Katie gets there and beats me to the shower. We'll never make it out tonight if you take as long as you did last weekend…"

"Can you just relax a second, babe?" Kyle said, turning back to me.

I was a bit blown away by all of this, and I squinted at him like I couldn't believe what I was seeing.

"Sorry, bud," he said. "Gotta run. You take care of yourself."

"You do the same," I said unenthusiastically. His M6 chirped rubber as he zipped out of the parking lot and weaved into the maze of traffic. I started walking again and spit into a storm drain. A bad taste had somehow filled my mouth during our conversation.

My cell phone rang.

"Hello?"

"Hey Adrian, it's Emily. Where are you?"

"I'm leaving school. Why? What's up?"

"You do any work on the résumé last night?"

"Yeah. I've done some stuff." I had spent about an hour the night before making minor changes, trying to figure out how to make it stand out.

"That's good. I snuck home some of my work from the recruiting office that I wanted to share with you. It's some more of that inner-circle stuff, if you know what I mean…"

"Cool. I'm game… I guess." I wasn't sure what Emily had up her sleeve, but I was intrigued.

"Yeah, you probably want to take a look at it. I think it will help you get your résumé up to snuff. You want to meet me at the coffee shop and we'll go over it?"

"Sounds good," I said. "I'll be there in 15."

"See you soon."

PART TWO

I met Emily at a small, privately owned coffee house called Caffeine Dream. Paul, the owner of the store took our orders.

Emily ordered first, "Can I get the turkey melt and a hot tea?"

"Sure," Paul said. "And you?" he pointed at me.

"Umm... I'll have the turkey melt as well."

"And to drink?"

I browsed his beverage selection, avoiding CommuniTea products. "Umm... Let me get a Pellegrino."

Paul typed it into the cash register and Emily paid.

"Thanks, Emily," I said, following her to the table.

"That's what friends are for."

"And thanks for letting me borrow your old notes for my cultural anthropology class," I said. "Professor Bryant speaks so quickly. I have a hard time getting it all down."

"Yeah, she sure knows how to rattle it off. Man..." she sighed, thinking back to her college days. "I haven't thought about that class in a while..."

"Bryant is still a bit crazy. She started talking about the term paper again today... even though we won't turn it in for another month or so."

"Her term papers are no joke. I spent several sleepless nights working on it, but I got a really good grade. I have it somewhere. I'll have to dig it out and let you look over it. I did mine on the ancient Native American story of the Alaskan Black Wolf."

"WHAT?" I yelled, busting out with laughter. "The *Alaskan Black Wolf*? What the hell is that?"

"What's so funny?"

"Um, nothing," I said, straightening my tone. She obviously didn't think it was at all comical. "I just thought the name sounded a bit... you know... hokey."

"It's a Native American name, Adrian. It's not *hokey*."

"I agree," I said. "Sounds like a great paper."

"Right… With all of the work you're doing researching and preparing for interviews, looking at my paper should help make your school workload a little less stressful."

"Yeah, that would be awesome. I'm kind of stuck deciding on what I want to write about." I suddenly remembered why we had come to the coffee shop and broke the conversation. School stuff could wait. "So, what did you bring home from the recruiting office?" I was still a bit skeptical about her ability to enhance my already *golden* résumé, but ever since the Suicide Caller stunt, I had become much more eager to get her advice.

"A bunch of stuff," she said, slapping a stack of documents on the table. "Read over each of these résumés and tell me what you like."

While I was reading, Paul delivered our sandwiches. We bit into our fresh panini. He sure made some delicious food…

I continued to study the résumés, holding them in my left hand while eating with my right. I studied… studied… there was nothing unusual, nothing exciting, nothing out of the ordinary.

"What am I supposed to learn from this? It looks just like mine."

"Keep reading them."

The next one was the same. "Emily, these are just like mine," I said. I began to feel pretty good about myself. Hell, my résumé was the same as the ones she had brought me to use as a model!

I read the third and the fourth. "Mine's even better than some of these!" I said.

"Tell me which one you would pick if you were an employer."

"Hmm…" I didn't know. I looked each one over. There was no difference. I hardly remembered one from another.

"What position are they applying for?"

"Good, I'm glad you asked. That's a question most people never think to ask. Résumés are *supposed* to be job specific. These people are applying for a sales position."

"Alright, sales it is…" I studied the résumés. "What would I be looking for if I was hiring a salesman…?" I continued to read through them. One guy was named Claude Nvarko. I remembered his résumé because he had such an unusual name. I set it aside.

"What's wrong with them?" she asked.

"Well, they're all pretty vague. This one just says, 'Excellent computer and typing skills.' What does that mean? Who doesn't have good typing skills?"

"And what else? Why can't you pick a winner?"

"I did. I picked Nvarko. He has a weird name. I like that. I want him on my team," I joked.

"Give me a break," she sipped on her tea. "What's the *problem* with that stack of résumés?"

"I guess none of them stand out."

"Why?"

"Well," I said, searching for the words. I had yet to totally wake up after Hackmuth's torturous lecture. "They're just very... vague. No real information is written. The responsibilities that they list seem impossible to visualize."

"Perfect," she said. "Why do you need to visualize what they have done?"

"If I knew the answer I wouldn't be having a hard time with it, now would I?" I said sarcastically.

"Fine. Let's look at this a different way. How do you measure success in school?"

I thought about it for a moment. "My GPA?"

"OK, good. How do you think a business measures its success?"

I felt like I should have known the answer to this question, but somehow I had no idea. "I guess it's how much revenue they bring in every year."

"Exactly. Every company's goal is to make as much money in as little time as possible. In order to do this, they need to hire people with a track record that shows they also value time and money."

"Makes sense," I agreed.

She stared pensively at the ceiling, thinking about how to word her lecture. "Write this down."

I took out a pen and notebook from my satchel and leaned onto the coffee table.

She began, "If you really want your résumé and cover letter to make an impact on the employer, you need to show them that you truly understand their core needs. In other words, you need to speak their language."

"How do I do that?"

"Good question. But before I tell you, you need to understand that this will *multiply* the level of success you have with your résumés by *at least* 10 times, if not more."

"Alright... well, let's hear it." I feigned skepticism, but beneath my sheen of confidence and reticence I was loaded with anticipation.

"Now then, in order for your résumé and cover letter to speak their language, you're going to need to address each of the *Three Pillars of Creating Key Contributions.*"

"Ok... and what are the 'Three Pillars of Creating Key Contributions'?" I signaled quotation marks in the air.

"I thought you'd never ask. The Three Pillars of Creating Key Contributions are:

I. Making Money
II. Saving Money
III. Saving Time

"Money is the lifeblood of a company. Without cash, these companies would go bankrupt and collapse. By presenting them with figures of your ability to save time and money, you're basically demonstrating to them that you're capable of 'supporting' the continuance of their survival. Do you follow?"

"Somewhat. I guess I'm just having a hard time wrapping my head around how I would actually go about showing this on my résumé."

"I've got you covered. I'm about to teach you a secret technique I call *Translating Your Contribution.*"

"Alright, Ace, slow down for a second." I was still writing the Three Pillars.

"The employer wants to see facts and figures. People like numbers. Do not include a bunch of descriptions. Instead, give them cold, hard, undeniable proof. Oftentimes, when individuals are generating material for their résumé, they write very vague, generalized responsibilities like, 'Maintained client files and databases' or 'monitored supplies and restocked when necessary.'"

"Right, like from the stack of résumés we looked at."

"Exactly. What these people should be doing is *Translating Their Contributions* by writing down concrete, measurable, tangible accomplishments or achievements. Doing this is what'll get you noticed—your ability to *Translate* your responsibilities into very specific accomplishments, or *Contributions* for the employer."

I stared at her blankly. I must have looked like a deer in headlights.

"Alright, I can see you're confused… Let me show you what I mean. In your experience at your last internship, when did you successfully save your company time and money?"

"Well, I didn't manage money. That wasn't in my job description."

"What were some of your responsibilities as an intern then? I'm your roommate, and I don't even know what you did at work."

I thought briefly and was drawing a blank. After a few more moments I finally came up with something. "I had to write and mail letters to customers thanking them for their continued business," I said. "See, that has nothing to do with money."

"Doesn't matter. You must have saved your company money somehow. How did you send the letters out?"

I closed my eyes and tried to imagine. "Well, I started out by addressing each letter individually."

"And did your process change? You said you started out doing that."

"Yeah, I learned how to do it a lot faster once I started using the Mail Merge feature."

"Bingo! See, you did save your company time. About how much time did you save using Mail Merge?"

"I dunno… probably seven and a half, maybe eight hours."

"And you were paid, what, $11 an hour?"

"Yeah."

"Alright, and how often did you have to do these mailings?"

"Once a month."

"So you sent out thank you letters twelve times a year, multiplied by the eight hours you saved each time, multiplied by your $11 per hour. (12 x 8 x 11 = $1,056.) You saved your company over a thousand dollars in one year. That's pretty impressive."

I had never thought of that before. On my résumé it merely said something like, "Organized files and documents." I recognized why this wouldn't mean anything. *Anyone* could say something like that. Not just anybody could save their company $1,056 in one year. It gave me an edge, and it gave me something to be remembered by.

"And what else?" she said, pointing at the résumés with her free hand. The tea was nearly empty. Paul walked over, a pitcher of hot water in his hand.

"Would you like more hot water? More tea?"

"Sure," Emily said.

He handed her another tea bag and filled her cup. "What are you two working on?" he asked, peering down at the résumés.

"She's helping me brush up my résumé," I said. "I'm about to apply for a job."

"You guys hire a lot of people, don't you?" Emily asked Paul.

"Sure, sure," Paul said, nodding his head.

"What do you look for when you're hiring a new employee?"

"Well, any barista that works here has to have very fine attention to detail. We're working with products that have expiration dates. We have to make sure we are providing our customers with fresh and safe products. We also have the health inspectors breathing down our necks, so I always look for someone who can keep the workplace clean and organized. What else... Oh yes, customer service is extremely vital to the success of our place. So, it stands to reason that I need a person who can keep up with the long line of customers during our lunch hours."

"How about with résumés and first impressions?" she prodded.

"I think that presentation is everything. A candidate really has to impress me, even before the interview begins. I always appreciate a well-organized résumé."

"Any specifics?"

"Basically, I look for someone who appears to be dependable and has the ability to get things done. Creativity is a plus in my book as well. I'm a pretty creative person, myself, as you can probably tell..." He ran his fingers through a set of thick dreadlocks. "Dependability and creativity are key attributes. They are what I look for most in a potential employee."

"Thanks, Paul," Emily said.

"No problem." He walked away, immediately striking up a conversation with another customer.

"So, what did you learn?" Emily asked.

"Nothing! I don't want to be a *barista*!"

"Jeez, Adrian, you're missing the point. The things he said apply to virtually every job scenario. Think about it: Dependability, cleanliness, organization, keeping up with customers during lunch hours... What do all of these things have in common?"

I was drawing another blank. "You got me..."

"Let me put it this way: What do you think would happen if Paul never cleaned up his shop and the health inspector stopped by?"

"He'd probably get fined," I said with confidence.

"Exactly. And what do you think would happen if he hired someone who was slow at cranking out sandwiches when hungry customers showed up during their lunch breaks?"

"The customers would probably leave."

"That's right. Are you starting to see how this is tying back to what we learned earlier? Making money, saving money, and saving time?"

I stared at the ceiling, trying to connect the dots in my head.

Emily continued, "If Paul got fined by the health department, his employees would've failed to help him save MONEY. And if one of Paul's employees failed to help him save TIME by making sandwiches faster, he would lose customers and as a result—fail to make MONEY. You get it?"

"OK, that makes sense. I think I get it." I thought about the analogy. I guess she was right, and maybe Paul had a bit more up his sleeve than I'd originally assumed. After all, he did own a successful coffee shop, which was much more than I could say for myself.

"Let's get back to all these résumés. Where did we leave off?" she asked.

"I was saying how similar they look to one another."

"Oh, right..." she smiled. She reached into her bag and removed a folder. She handed it to me. "Remember what Paul just told us? Now take a look at *this* one."

I removed a piece of paper from the folder. "Wow," I said, studying the new résumé. "It's colorful." I scanned down the page noticing a wide array of different graphics and additions that were absent on most conventional résumés. "Who made this?"

"It's a mockup I've made for myself. It's as close to *perfect* as you can get."

"Man... it really is." I studied the facts and figures, the numbers, the graphics, the testimonials... all of it had been organized so well. "Do you always put graphics like this?" I pointed at the string of graphics running down the side of the page.

"The human mind recognizes graphics and images faster than it can recognize words, sounds, even odors. If you include an image like the one at the top there—it's my alma mater's seal—you're going to interest the employer right off the bat. Everyone knows that college is a huge plus to getting almost *any* job, so putting your school's emblem at the top of the résumé shows that you're proud of your education and take it very seriously. Just be careful that it doesn't look like a letterhead, because you don't want the employer to think that your school is contacting them."

"Right, right…" I studied the résumé. Instead of bullets beside each accomplishment or skill, Emily had put check marks. I asked her about why she chose these marks instead of bullets or dashes.

"I call this the *Check-Vibing Technique*."

"Check-Vibing, huh? What does that mean?"

"It's all about the check marks. Check marks give positive vibes," she took another sip of her tea. "Ever since elementary school we got check marks on our papers when we passed a test, and minus marks when we failed."

I thought back to the last time I got a check mark and recalled the feelings I got from seeing the symbol.

"Wow, that's kind of cool."

"I know, right? You're tapping-in to *decades* of subconscious social programming and visual recognition." She smiled and nodded. "You didn't know it went that deep, did you?"

"I guess I never thought about it."

"And remember what we were talking about with facts and figures?" she asked. "Go ahead and read through mine."

I read the Key Accomplishments section of her résumé. Emily had done some pretty amazing stuff, and some of the things I hadn't even heard about. For instance, she had saved her company $15,000 and established over 120 new clients, all during the first three weeks of her employment. Several months later she took a new position managing a team of eight. Their team was responsible for planning, organizing, and hosting four large benefit galas over a period of one year.

"Wow," I said, still reading. "I never knew you did all *this*! You're kind of a badass, aren't you?"

She laughed at me. "I wouldn't go that far, but I certainly give my company everything I've got."

"These are just so detailed and specific," I said. "It's very professional looking… very concise… or, rather, *precise*."

"It's both. You're exactly right. You see, employers want to see figures. Dollar amounts, percentages, time frames, any *numbers* that you've got, they want. The more you can quantify it, the better. At the end of the day, employers are concerned with saving money, saving time, and most importantly, making money. You have to remember that."

"That's the truth," I said. "Honestly, even after all these years of college, I had never thought of it like that."

"I know, neither have most college students. That's the problem. That's why most people can't get the jobs they want—because our educational system doesn't actually teach you how to do it." She shook her head thoughtfully, reverting back to our original conversation. "The more you can convey that you are capable of doing those things that I mentioned, the more interested they'll be in interviewing you and ultimately giving you the job." She picked up my résumé. "From looking at your first draft, it's clear you need to incorporate more numbers and figures into your achievements. They're coming off a little lackluster. You've got the right idea, but you need to beef up your appeal with numbers. I call this the Naked Proof Technique."

"Sounds good," I said, trying to absorb all of this information.

"I want you to look at something on our way out of here." We stood up, gathering our things to leave the shop. She stopped beside Paul's main cooler and pointed at a bottle of juice called *Naked*.

"I've had a bottle of that before," I said. "It's awesome."

"People love it," Emily said. "Did you know Naked Juice bumped Odwalla Juice from virtually all Starbucks coffee shops?"

"Really? I had no idea."

"Why do you suppose it happened?"

I thought about it. "Because all the hippies found out that Odwalla was owned by Coke?"

"No..." Emily took out the juice container from the cooler and handed it to me.

"Hmmm...Mighty Mango," I said still curious about where she was going with this.

"Take a look at the back of the bottle. See how it lists *exactly* what's inside each bottle? Looks like this one contains 2 ½ mangoes, ¾ of a banana, 2 oranges, 3 ½ apples, and a hint of lemon."

"Yeah, that's kinda cool. It's hard to believe there are so many pieces of fruit in this tiny little bottle."

"I know, right? This company eliminates all of the guesswork and cuts right to the chase. It's BRILLIANT marketing."

"So what does this have to do with Naked Juice replacing Odwalla Juice?"

"More people were buying Naked Juice than Odwalla. I mean, would you want to replace a product that was already bringing in lots of money with another product that didn't bring in as much money?"

"Not if I wanted to be profitable."

"Exactly. So this is why you should use the same *proven* strategy on your résumé. After all, if it works for a multi-million-dollar corporation like Naked Juice, you can sure as hell bet it'll work for you."

I bobbed my head up and down while reading the back of the bottle. I was impressed and suddenly felt much better about my chances of getting a good job. Emily's "crazy" tactics were beginning to make sense.

PART THREE

W e parked on the street outside of the apartment and walked inside together. We spent a half hour organizing a new rough draft of my résumé, implementing all of the tricks she'd taught me at Caffeine Dream.

After we drew up a rough draft, I spent about an hour and a half re-organizing, editing, and adding information. When I felt like it was solid, I called Emily downstairs to check it out.

"Looks good..." she said, reading carefully with her finger beside each check mark.

"Color, lots of graphics, no giant text blocks, no useless information... it's definitely NOT conventional."

"You did a good job leaving out unimportant information. Here, hang it on the wall." She took tape from her desk drawer and attached a piece to the top of the page.

"Awww... are you so proud of me that you're going to hang it on the wall?" I mocked her.

"No, you idiot, I'm checking to see if it's balanced. You should always tape your résumé to the wall, stand back, and look at it from a distance."

"What the hell for? Is this something you learned from Josh's art class on Thursday nights?" Emily had often thought of attending one of Josh's painting classes, and I made it a point to jab her about it whenever I could. Not that Josh was a bad painter, just that Emily was, well... never mind.

"I happen to be quite good at this."

"What is *this*? What are you looking for?"

"Are there any blank spaces? Is everything balanced? Are your margins too wide or too narrow? You should ask yourself questions like these after every revision. I have to say, though, yours doesn't look too bad..."

"I think I got this thing looking pretty good. I think this thing is ready to take on Empyrean."

"Hold your horses, Desperado. Let's try Proteus & Paulson first. I think you need a trial run to see how the thing works."

"OK, OK… They're not accepting applications yet anyway. I'll just try Proteus & Paulson."

"My money says you'll get a callback. They'll be sure to give you a ring after you wow them with the amount of research you've done. Oh, and here, take this." She handed me a thin black plastic rectangle.

"What is it? A flash drive?"

"No, it's called a TuneTalk. Plug it into your iPod, then slip your iPod into your breast pocket during the interview. You'll be able to record everything that is said. This way we can review the interview when you get home."

"Thanks, Em," I said, studying the tiny device. "Alright, I guess I'm going to lock myself in my room and not come out until I know *everything* about P&P."

"Sounds good. I hope you're finished by Saturday."

"What do you mean?"

"You don't remember?" I had no idea what she was talking about. "There's that volunteering opportunity I told you about."

"But I told you I had—"

She cut me off. "I know you said you have plans or whatever, but if you really want to land Empyrean, you'll come with me."

"What are we doing?"

"You'll see…"

*   *   *

Emily and I approached a very tall glass building. She led me through the front doors, beneath a sign that read:

CHARITY | WELLS
FOUNDATION

"I've heard of this before," I said.

"Have you?"

"Yeah… these guys drill wells in African countries so that people don't have to walk 10 miles just to get potable drinking water."

"That's right," she said. "It was founded by Bill Blanchard and Robert West. Robert West is the guy walking toward us right now."

I saw a man headed across the marble floored lobby. He was tall, well-built, with dark hair and glasses. He seemed energetic and youthful despite being in his mid-forties.

"He sorta looks like Hugh Grant from *Notting Hill*," I said softly.

She chuckled. "Robert is a *very* successful marketer. I've learned a lot from him over the past few years."

"Emily! How's it going? I see you've brought a friend?" Robert said, hugging Emily and extending a hand toward me.

"This is Adrian Addler, my roommate." We shook hands.

"Nice to meet you, Adrian."

"Adrian's in the middle of a hectic job search," Emily explained. "I brought him along to get his mind on something other than work."

"Sounds good to me," Robert said. "Well, Emily, take our friend Adrian into the arena." He pointed to a glass room filled with cubicles and telephones. Seven or eight people were inside wearing earpieces and looking at computer screens. Emily led me in and explained the task: Raise as much money for *Charity | Wells* as possible. She sat down, immediately making her first call and successfully getting a $100 donation.

"That's how you do it," she said.

It took me several tries, but after a while I was raising a fair amount of money. At the end of three hours my total was up to $200.

"Not bad," Robert West said.

"I'll do better next time."

"Sounds good to me," he laughed. "Hey, Emily," he tapped her on the shoulder. She was still reading something on the computer screen. "I need somebody to baby-sit my kids the Friday after next? Does that sound good to you?"

"Yeah," she said. "I think so. Let me check."

"Cool. I'm going out of town to see Elaine and I need somebody to hang out at the house."

"I'm pretty sure that will work."

"Just give me a call and let me know."

After a few more minutes we made our exit from *Charity | Wells*. In the car Emily explained that she could not babysit Robert's kids. She had plans to take a vacation that week.

"What the hell did you lie to him for?"

"I didn't lie. He said he needed *somebody* to stay with his kids. I know *somebody* who can..." she looked at me.

"What? He didn't say that! And why would I want to do that anyway? Are you crazy? Why would *you* ever do something like that? You're a successful career person, why are you babysitting kids on a Friday night?"

"It's not about money, Adrian. You definitely have something to gain by babysitting for Robert West."

"Like what? What could I possibly gain from this?"

*   *   *

The following week, roughly three days after emailing my résumé, I got a phone call from Proteus & Paulson. They conducted a brief phone interview and asked me to come down for a face-to-face. Wow, this had all happened very fast...

The following morning I put on my suit, drove down there on my last half-tank of gas, and parked my dusty old car in the rear of the lot. I got out and straightened my hair in the reflection of an SUV's window. I checked my teeth.

"AH!" I jumped back and screamed, a giant bulldog lashed at the window. It startled me so much that I actually started shaking. I walked into the building, still wide-eyed, and greeted the receptionist. She told me to take a seat. I sat down and reached into my breast pocket. I had almost forgotten to turn on my TuneTalk.

"Adrian Addler?" A man with glasses asked. He had thick hands and a thick voice and was much larger than me. I shook his hand, felt it crush my own, and followed him down the hallway toward the interrogation room—I mean the *interviewing* room.

"I'm Steve Williams. I'll be interviewing you today," he said as we walked. "So, how are the last few weeks treating you?"

"Good..." I said, having no idea what he meant.

"I'm meant school," he laughed. "How's it going?"

I suddenly felt very nervous, like I'd been embarrassed or humiliated in front of a group of people. I couldn't explain it, but my tongue actually felt larger and I couldn't enunciate clearly (or at least I felt like I couldn't). "Oh, right, school... It's going good. Very good." I lied. School was horrible, of course. I had so many projects due, so many tests coming up... it was a nightmare just keeping it all straight.

We entered the room together and he took a seat behind the desk. "Alright, Adrian, so how about starting from the beginning. Can you tell me a little bit about yourself?"

"Well, let's see... I was born in the Midwest. I'm an only child. I spent most of my life in Indiana. When I was 16 my family moved here for my father's job. I applied to the university, was accepted to my department of choice, and worked like a dog to maintain excellent grades all the way through."

"Interesting," Steve said, taking no notes and staring pensively into my soul.

"And from there... Well, you see, I always wanted to study business. And..." I was stumbling, looking all over the room as though I were looking for hidden answers written on the wall. "Well, I chose this industry because I projected that I would end up with a good job after I graduated. It turned out that I got a great internship, worked there for a year, expected to get a career out of it..." I shook my head, remembering the previous month. "But they had to cut my position for budgetary reasons."

"Look at you now," Steve said, pointing around the office. "You're moving up in the world." He laughed, insinuating that P&P was better than whatever I'd been doing before.

"I agree," I said enthusiastically. "I've got my sights set on going *up*." My eyes met his, and I quickly looked away. For some reason I felt very uneasy about making eye contact with him. "And I guess that brings us up to date. Here I am, ready to begin a career."

"Very good," he said. Very good. It meant that I was getting somewhere. It wasn't just a "good" or an "OK." It was "very good." But, then again, his heart wasn't in it. He glanced down at my résumé, still very emotionless. They trained guys like him to behave this way. It was a torture tactic. You could never read them.

"What interests you about this field?"

My heart pounded against my chest. It was the same unexplainable nervousness that had seized me earlier. I had not expected such a simple question. I had only researched the answers to the tough, in-depth questions. I racked my brain for a response.

"Well, my heart was set on the university, and they definitely have one of the best business schools in the country, so it seemed like a perfect pairing." Whew. I hoped that was a sufficient answer.

He briefly contemplated this before moving on to his next question.

"What are the top duties you perform in your current or most-recent position?"

I hesitated, trying to think back to what I did the last time I was at my internship. I replied, rather unsure, "Mainly document organization and assisting the project team with stuff like sending out invoices or letters, making copies, and processing paper work."

"What is the most significant project or suggestion you have initiated in your career?"

The questions came faster than bullets. I stuttered, licked my lips, and tried to come up with an answer. I drew a blank. "Well… I've done several things at my internship that were significant. I've organized several project teams and made some strides others thought were impossible."

"I see…"

The questions went on and on… for nearly 40 minutes. Finally, I heard resolution in his voice, as though the interrogation was coming to a close. "Alright," he said, striking his pen on the paper. "Do you have any questions for me?"

I tried to think, but something froze up inside of me. "Well, honestly, I don't think so. You've been very thorough."

We stood, him slightly ahead of me, and shook hands. He pointed the way out. I glided onto the elevator, reaching in my breast pocket to see the time display on my TuneTalk: 46 minutes 12 seconds. Three quarters of an hour of pure, unabridged questioning. I felt like a prisoner of war who had just been released, as I leaned one arm on the elevator wall and sighed with relief.

*   *   *

Emily was at Josh's place and I found myself wanting to talk about the interview. I gave Jake a call, but he didn't answer. Instead of thinking about jobs I decided to surf the internet for a while and look up workout routines. I had been in the gym a lot recently, and I had discovered how liberating weight lifting really was. There was something very Zen about the whole thing, something that kept me going back. It was a good break from work, and an excellent way for me to clear my head and focus on getting my priorities straight.

I was watching a three-minute Ronnie Coleman (pro bodybuilder) video, which was really insane and hilarious at the same time, when my cell phone rang. I didn't even bother to look at who it was.

"Hello?"

"Hey, Adrian, it's Dad." I quickly moved the phone away from my ear and mouthed the word *shit*. I should've checked the caller ID...

"Hey Dad, what's up?" I knew he was going to ask me about my job search.

"Not much, how are things going for you? How's the job search coming?"

"Well, strange you should ask, I just got out of my first interview."

"That's really good. How did it go?"

"It went alright, I think. I stumbled on a few questions, but overall the guy seemed really interested in what I had to say."

"You made sure to ask when they were going to call back, didn't you?"

I was silent. I had forgotten.

"Adrian... come on, bud. You gotta be on point in these interviews if you want to—"

"I know, I know..." I had heard all of this before. "...if I want to get ahead in this economy. I got it, Dad."

"Relax, Adrian. What's gotten in to you?"

"I'm sorry. I'm just a bit stressed from all this job hunting. I'm trying to relax tonight, but I keep thinking about everything."

"It's fine... So, did you ask them any other questions?"

"No, not really. The guy was pretty thorough." I tried to play this off like it didn't matter. Big mistake. I could tell right away that I was in for the lecture of the century from the World's Greatest Interviewer. And, hell, I couldn't disparage him. He had great job security, always had, always maintained a strong work ethic, and everyone I'd ever known had only good things to say about him.

"You know that employers like it when you ask questions. It makes you seem much more interested in the position. Even if they've gone over almost everything, you should always try to find something to ask."

"I know, I know..." I said. "I just couldn't think of something on the spot like that."

"Well, you should try to think of that stuff beforehand. When I was your age, we would write down—"

"Questions on note cards and practice them… I know, Dad. I've *heard.*"

He laughed. "Sorry, bud. You know I only want you to have a successful life."

"I know. It's fine. Thank you."

"So, overall you think it went well?"

There was a moment of silence while I remembered the interview, wondering: Had it really gone *that* well? I quickly dispelled my doubts. Of course it had gone well. This was Adrian Addler we were talking about! If there was one thing I was good at, it was going face-to-face with an employer.

"Yeah, it went well overall."

"Good. Keep me posted," Dad said. "Let me know when they call back."

"Will do. What are you up to?"

"Your mother and I are about to go out for our anniversary dinner." He chuckled. "Thanks for the card and phone call…"

"Ah, shoot… Dad, I'm sorry. I totally forgot…"

"It's fine, it's fine. I never remembered my parents' anniversary either. Few people do."

"Yeah, but I should have had it written down or something." I ran my fingers through my hair, feeling stupid. "Happy anniversary." I futilely added.

"Thanks," he said. "Remember to keep us posted. I'm serious, too. Your mother and I want to take you out to celebrate as soon as you find out."

"Alright Dad…" I sighed. "I'll call you the minute I hear from them."

IT'S NOT THE STRONGEST OF
THE SPECIES, NOR THE MOST
INTELLIGENT, THAT SURVIVE;
IT'S THE ONE MOST
RESPONSIVE TO CHANGE.

....

–CHARLES DARWIN
Evolutionary Biologist and English Naturalist

CHAPTER 3

UNFAMILIAR TERRITORY

A week passed by with relative ease. School had become a semi-unimportant backdrop, an impertinent prop in the far rear of my job-hunting life. I had managed to get three phone interviews during the week, and I had good feelings about all of them. Well… two of them, anyway.

My first phone interview had been with a smaller firm called Potter & Sons, which has an amazing reputation. My second phone interview was with the Bauer Consulting Managers. This was supposed to be a really big one for me, but it didn't go exactly as planned. Jake had been at my apartment the day of the interview. He came over to watch a basketball game since his cable hadn't been working. While I was speaking with Bauer Consulting Managers on the phone, Jake was overcome by a disagreement with one of the ref's calls…

I was speaking to the Consulting Managers, having a great conversation. For the first time in all of these attempts, things were actually going smoothly. "Do I have experience? Yes, sir," I said. "I have been working in this industry as an intern for—"

A shriek from the other room interrupted my sentence. It was Jake's voice yelling, "You chubby son of a bitch! You've probably never played a game of basketball in your life! No wonder you're calling fouls! You're a fairy! You're a damn #%$#%$!"

Needless to say, the Bauer Consulting Managers never followed up with me. Leave it to Jake, the guy who's already got his job in the bag, to muck up interviews for the rest of us.

My silver lining came with a call from Farnam Partners, the fourth company on my top-15 list. I had sent in a résumé and cover letter and received a call from them only two days later. This time, I made sure Jake wasn't around to screw things up. I impressed them enough to be invited in for a face-to-face interview. Potter & Sons had also decided to have me come in for an interview. I was finally beginning to see some progress from all of my hard work.

*   *   *

Jake was coming to my place from school to drink some beers. It was Friday afternoon and I was tired, in no mood to drink beers, but Jake was my best friend.

I needed a meal. I told Jake this and he called me a wimp, made fun of me for being uninterested in drinking.

"I just don't have as tough of a stomach," I said.

"It's cool, man. Here, let's go into the burrito joint."

We walked inside, and without asking, he paid for my burrito. "Thanks, man. I'll get you back as soon as I get some funds put back into my account."

"It's no big deal," he said. "It's the least I can do for screwing up your interview. I feel bad, but what can you do? The NBA just isn't what is used to be. That ref, pardon my French, was a clueless son of a..."

"Thanks for the apology," I said, shaking my head and laughing under my breath. "And thanks for the burrito."

We walked down the street and into my house. He reached into my fridge and pulled out a near-empty bottle of rum.

"Rum?" he said, disgusted. "I hate rum. What else you got?"

"It's that or Keystone."

"Where's the beer?"

"Bottom shelf, vegetable drawer."

He opened the drawer and fished out two beers.

"I don't want one," I said.

He chuckled and set the beers on the counter, cracked the first, chugged it, and then cracked the second.

"I'm going down to that thing at Mallory's place tonight. That party or whatever. You coming?"

"Um..." I said, stalling. I didn't want to tell him that I had to babysit for Robert West. "I don't really feel much like partying tonight."

The front door flew open and Emily gusted through the kitchen. "Hi, boys, how's it going?"

"Fine, Emily. How are you? Let me get that bag for you," Jake said, ever so sleazily. He loved to flirt with her, especially if I was around.

Emily disappeared up the staircase and into her room. Jake followed with the bag. She was always in a hurry, but always so relaxed about being in a hurry.

A few moments later, I heard them laughing, her slapping him, and then her door closing. He came down the staircase with a smile like he'd just been knocked in the head. He stood there silently, daydreaming. "That girl is something else…"

"What about her?"

"It's just… you know…" Jake lowered his voice so Emily wouldn't hear upstairs. "What I wouldn't give to tap that... even just once."

"Dude—Not cool!" I nearly shouted, but remembered that Emily was in the house. I whispered to him, "Jake, she's practically like a *sister* to me!"

"There's no rule saying I can't be in love with your sister…" He whistled, still imagining Emily's body or face or whatever. "You're something else," I said. "Just *try* to keep your thoughts to yourself."

"I'm sorry dude," he laughed, "but she's got to be one of the hottest chicks in this city."

"Alright, Jake… I get it," I said sternly.

Emily came back into the kitchen and removed a bottle of water from the fridge. "Starting early, huh?" she laughed, noticing the two beer cans on the table.

"It's Friday," Jake said. "You want one?"

"They're MY beers," Emily laughed. "But thanks for offering."

Jake continued to drink and Emily turned to me. "Come in here for a minute, Adrian." She took me into the living room and we sat on the couch. She produced an envelope from a stack of papers in her hand. It was from Proteus & Paulson.

"Sweet," I said. "That was pretty fast."

"Open it."

I opened it. For some reason I couldn't read it, I just stared at the text and scanned up and down.

"Hmm…" I said, beginning the letter at the top. It was plain to see from the first few lines that I had failed. The job was going to someone else. I read through the letter, searching for a meaning, a reason why, some sort of explanation. There was nothing.

"I thought I did so well…"

Jake came into the living room and took a seat in the easy chair. He turned on the television. The noise was so loud from the TV that he couldn't hear us.

"It's OK, Adrian..." Emily said. "Don't let it get you down." She ran her fingers through her hair.

"I don't know what I'm going to do. I can't even get an offer at P&P. How am I going to get a job at Empyrean? I've borrowed money from my parents for rent. Jake has bought me lunch three separate times... I thought that my interviewing skills were improving. I can't keep living this way." I looked over to make sure that Jake wasn't paying attention. He had an unlit cigarette hanging out of his mouth and was staring at the TV.

I snapped back to reality. I had totally bombed my interview at P&P. I was so embarrassed. "I just don't know where I could have gone wrong. The interviewer kept asking me questions for a solid 45 minutes, and I answered every single one."

"Well, of course you answered every single one. You'd be a fool not to. Plus, all of the practicing you did paid off, right?"

"Kind of. This sounds stupid, but they asked some pretty simple questions that I hadn't even thought of during my preparation."

"What kind of questions?" Emily asked, looking a little disappointed that I had been so naive as to overlook the simplest questions.

"Well, he started out the interview by asking me why I chose this field for my career. Who asks a question like that? What am I supposed to say, 'I just picked it out of a hat in fourth grade?' I didn't think I needed a reason."

"I hope you came up with a better response than that!"

"Of course I did. But then he asked me where I saw myself in five years. It took me a few moments to come up with an answer since I'd never thought about it before, but I finally said something like, 'I'd like to have your position in five years.'"

Emily looked shocked. "That's it? That's all you said?"

"Pretty much. I figured he'd be impressed with my confidence. But now that I think about it, maybe I shouldn't have said that. I guess I just couldn't put where I wanted to be into words fast enough. Like I said, the question caught me off guard."

Emily shook her head from side to side, then took a deep breath. "Well, since we can't change the past, there's no use dwelling over this any more than we need to. So long as you've learned a valuable lesson from this experience." She stared pensively into my eyes, waiting for me to recite the lesson.

I shrugged my shoulders and replied, "Don't use that line anymore?"

Emily slapped her palm against her forehead. I could tell she was getting frustrated with me. "Adrian, do you have a clear goal in mind?"

"What do you mean? Of course I do. I want to get a job." I thought it was obvious by now.

"That's not what I mean. Let me rephrase my question: Do you know how successful you want to be? Where do you ideally want to be in 30 years?"

I didn't know how to answer that question. "Well, umm... I want to be financially secure I guess. Maybe start my own business? I like the idea of being my own boss."

"And how are you going to ensure that this happens?"

"Well, I guess I need to start with getting some real-world experience. Make sure I get a job with a reputable company that I can see myself staying with for several years and learning the ropes."

"Sounds like a good answer, but where are you going to get this job?"

"With any luck it'll be with Empyrean."

"Why Empyrean?"

I was getting frustrated with Emily. She kept asking me these stupid questions, but I knew it was for a reason... I just didn't know what it was.

"I guess I'd have to say it's because Empyrean is the best company in the field. Word on the street is that entry-level positions at Empyrean are way better in the long run than entry-level jobs elsewhere, because of the responsibilities you get from day one."

"But, do you think you're up to the challenge? It sounds like you would have a lot of competition applying for this job as well as working for the company."

"I like competition," I said. "I've heard if you could survive two years at Empyrean, you'll be able to survive anywhere. Just think of how much I will know after working with those people..."

Emily breathed a sigh of relief. "Finally, we got there! Don't you see Adrian? You want to work for the best in the field so you can *learn* from the best. Next time you get asked the question 'Where do you see yourself in 5 years?' try to relate it back to what you want to have *learned* by then. You need to be clear about your purpose. Remember this: Clear visions create causes. You need to visualize what you want before you can actually achieve it. If you don't know your destination, it doesn't much matter which way you go."

Emily paused for several seconds before continuing, "I'm going to share a secret with you. You have to keep it quiet, though... not everyone can know that I did this."

"What? What the hell are you talking about? What kind of secret?"

Jake looked over at us. "You guys seen *Pineapple Express* yet? It's in stores. I thought about picking it up today. Either of you want to watch it?"

"No," I said. "I've got stuff going on."

"Emily?" he prodded.

"Maybe later," she said.

"I'll hold you to that," he smiled and winked at her.

She laughed. "Alright," she continued, grabbing my arm. "Come in the kitchen."

I followed her in there. "What secret are you talking about?"

"You're going to baby-sit Robert's kids tonight, right?"

"Yeah?"

"You're in for a real treat."

"What do you mean?"

"Robert is a marketing genius. In fact, people call him The Marketer. That's how good he is."

"OK... and what does this have to do with me?"

"You're babysitting his kids, Adrian. It will give you a chance to ask for his advice about—" Jake blurted out laughter from the other room and came traipsing into the kitchen. He looked at us strangely, grabbed a third beer, and headed back to his chair.

Emily continued, "The way it usually works is I look after Robert's kids in exchange for his giving me a few tips for my own profession. I think he'd be very willing to do the same for you."

"OK, so what do I do? Just watch the kids and then when he gets home I ask him how I should go about getting a job?" I laughed. It seemed ridiculous.

"I'll call him and explain everything. He'd be more than happy to help you."

We walked back into the living room. The envelope from P&P was lying on the table, torn apart like road kill. Jake asked about it. I told him that it was junk mail and shoved it deep into the trashcan. I stood there in a daze, staring blankly at the television. Emily was in the other room on the phone. She came back into the den.

"I know you're a bit skeptical, Adrian, but Robert knows his stuff. He's been known to charge up to $20k a day for his consulting services. In essence, you're getting a $5,000 tutorial for one night of your time."

"Sounds good to me."

She handed me a piece of paper with the directions already typed out. "It's the tan house with a black Cadillac in the driveway. You can't miss it."

"Alright."

I sat down on the couch beside Jake.

"You want to get drunk tonight or what?" he asked.

"I actually can't. I'm going over to this girl's house a bit later." Good thinking, Adrian... This way I'd keep the secret and seem like a badass all at the same time.

"What? What girl? You didn't mention this?"

"That girl from Hackmuth's class. You've seen her. Lacy Ashford."

"The one with the huge rack?"

"I guess you could say that." I nodded, pretending to be imagining the beautiful future that lay before me. In a way, I guess I was.

"You're going over to her house? Tonight? To sit around in her bedroom or what?"

"Don't have any idea. Just going over there, man. She told me she wanted me to."

"Damn... that's awesome."

I smiled and walked into the pale lighted kitchen. This was another chance for me to make something of myself. I grabbed a piece of pizza from the refrigerator and ate it without a plate.

PART TWO

I arrived at Robert West's place and parked beside the lone black Cadillac. I walked to the front door and knocked. It flung open. There was no one in the foyer.

"Hello?" I called.

A boy jumped out from behind the door and made a face at me. He screamed playfully and ran up the stairs. I took a hesitant step inside and called out for Mr. West.

"One second," he said, yelling from a different part of the house. "Come inside, come inside!"

I walked in and shut the door. The place was flawlessly decorated, with beautiful rugs over hardwood floors and a crystal chandelier hanging high above my head. I could see into the other room. A little girl was playing with a set of dolls. Several toy swords were strewn across the dining room table and a giant fluffy cat was asleep on the floor. No one seemed to notice me for several minutes.

"Adrian," Robert smiled, floating down the staircase with his hand extended. "How are you? Emily told me you'd be coming. Sorry I wasn't down here; I'm just running on the edge of my schedule."

"That's fine," I said. I followed him into the kitchen. "I like your house. You've got a great sense of style."

"Thanks." He opened a folder on the counter and read over some stuff. "Everything you need to know should be written down in here. If it's not, here are the numbers to my cell, my sister's house, the neighbor's houses, and even a couple more. None of the kids have any health conditions or anything, so you should be good to go."

I nodded at him. He must have really trusted Emily in order to blindly accept me as her replacement. I guess people knew that Emily was a good person. Maybe they could sense something from me as well. I hoped so.

"So, you're heading out of town for the night?"

"Yeah, something like that." He winked at me. "I got a date with a woman who lives two hours away. I've been out with her for about a year and I'm thinking to myself: She's is the one." He laughed. "Anyway, I need somebody to help me take care of these animals." He pointed at the floor. There was a green dinosaur eating a Spiderman action figure. A little boy flew through the room like a bat out of hell, not even noticing the toys that he'd left lying in his wake.

"I gotta run. I'll be home tomorrow around noon or maybe a bit later."

"Have a good time. Everything will be fine here."

"Oh, shoot," he said. "I didn't introduce you to the animals themselves…"

He called the kids into the kitchen and we were briefly introduced. Two boys and one girl. It would be pretty simple, he assured me. All I had to do was maintain control…

And with that Robert walked out the front door and slid into his car.

PART THREE

The morning came without serious incident and I awoke to the sound of children's voices. The kids had begun moving with the first indication of dawn. They ran up and down the stairs, picking up where they had left off the day before. I got out several bowls, poured cereal, called them into the kitchen, and we ate together. One happy family.

"I hope Emily's being serious," I said to myself. "I hope that this guy can tell me what I need to know." I had every reason to believe that he could. Look at his house, his car, his charitable work, the way he was willing to drive two hours just for a date.

The kids continued to play, sleep, and scream at one another, and at noon we ate lunch. Robert showed up as I was putting the plates in the dishwasher.

"How were they?" he asked.

"Good. There weren't any problems."

"Great. How's your job search going?"

"Yeah, it's going alright."

He must have picked up on my uneasiness.

"Emily told me you had some trouble at P&P?"

"It wasn't the application... it was more the interview. They called me in to talk, but I must have made a mistake."

He took me into the other room. His 17" Aluminum Macbook Pro gleamed from the top of a lacquered mahogany desk. I had always wanted one of those computers...

"Check this out," he opened up a webpage. "What do you think of this site? Be honest. Be brutally honest."

I looked at the webpage. It was simple, too simple. "I looks like a scam or something. Like someone assembled it on the spur of the moment."

"Exactly. That's how you probably looked to employers." He clicked another link and a new page opened. "How about this one?"

"Well, it's the same company... but it looks really good. It looks much better, in fact. There's more color, the graphics have been improved, the text is bigger, the testimonials are better." I noticed check marks beside several of the company's achievements. Now I knew where Emily had been pulling her information. She was such a clever girl. "What do you think about testimonials?" I asked.

"Testimonials are a marketer's greatest weapon. They instill trust into people."

I nodded, trying to understand what he meant.

"When you see other people who are similar to you (age, personality, etc.) saying good things about the product you're thinking of buying, your natural tendency is to be more trusting of the product. Wouldn't you agree?"

"Yeah," I said.

"Why do you think Amazon and Netflix started using the customer reviews on their websites? Because people are more likely to buy something if they find even one review that is written from the perspective of a buyer they can relate to."

"That makes sense. I always look for online reviews of products before I buy them."

"Exactly. And here's a helpful tip: If you're going to put a testimonial on your résumé, find someone who is in a management role. The higher the seniority, the better."

"Got it," I said, studying the document on his screen.

"This looks much better, doesn't it?"

"Yeah."

"And that's how Emily has probably taught you to format your résumé, right? That's why you got called back for that job at P&P."

"I guess so."

"And then you botched the interview because you didn't know how to back it up. They had all this hype surrounding your résumé, and then BAM—you walked in there and the whole thing blew up in your face."

"It wasn't that bad, but yeah…"

"It was that bad," he said. "There are seldom any that are good. Unless you know how to get into their heads."

"What do you mean?"

"Out back," he motioned toward the window. "It's pool time."

We went into the kitchen and he ushered the children, already in their bathing suits, into the backyard. They ran into the water like seals, swimming and splashing one another wildly.

He poured us both glasses of ice water. It was a perfect day and I had a feeling, an easy and wonderful feeling that I was finally going to learn everything I needed to know.

"First things first: I'm going to tell you something that most people don't know about interviewing. Call it an unspoken rule of getting hired if you will. It goes like this: Getting the Interview = Marketing Yourself. Think about it: If you know you want to buy a TV, what do you think Best Buy does to get you to come and look at *their* TVs instead of another company's?"

"They advertise?"

"That's right! And that's exactly what you need to do in order to land the interview. You need to advertise or market yourself. Only instead of using newspapers, use your résumé and cover letter."

"Right…" I thought about all the things Emily had said about my résumé. I was beginning to realize how crucial a role my résumé played in getting a job.

"I'm going to give you a little history lesson. It's something that you haven't learned in school, and it's going to help you understand how to better formulate your strategy."

"Alright, shoot."

"Well, Adrian, this society is the first ever 'over-communicated' society in the history of our world. Let me explain it this way: When most people think of marketing, they think of big-business marketing: 'Let's try to get our brand name and logo out there and seen by as many people as possible.' Of course, big business can afford marketing this way, and it worked in the industrial age. However, in the information age, in order to stand out, it's become more complicated than simply spamming out a bunch of flyers or getting on TV."

I nodded and he took a sip of his water.

"You see, Adrian, successful marketers need to be a little more street smart than everyone else. The marketing world, and consequently the interviewing world, evolved from getting your name OUT there," he pointed away from him, "to getting other's perspective IN here." He pointed at his chest. Think of it as using a sniper rifle instead of a shotgun. Remember: 'He who chases two rabbits catches none.'

"It's because most people see the hiring process as a monotonous, 'throw everything at the wall and see what sticks' process. That's exactly what they teach you in school, and that's how I did it when I graduated. And because of this belief, these people approach their job hunt with a 'numbers game' mentality. They end up working harder and harder at finding a job instead of taking a step back and working smarter.

"I remember when I was about your age and looking for my first job. I applied to as many jobs as I could. I interviewed at every chance. I did this every day without exception. I looked at every resource I could find. And I spent hours each day reformatting my résumé to the point of insanity. I think I submitted 87 résumés (yes, 87… I counted) to companies who were looking to hire college students with my specific major. I waited and waited but had no luck.

"Don't get me wrong; to a certain extent, it is a numbers game, but all too many people make the mistake of thinking that's the only key to getting a job: Apply to every company looking to hire. It would be like if you were at a bar trying to get a girl's number, and instead of picking one girl you simply asked every girl you saw. Think about how many times you would have to be turned down until one of them actually gave it to you."

"Probably a lot of times."

"Exactly. You would have a very poor chance of succeeding. And who knows if it would even be a real number or not. Now, what if I told you the way to do this is to have a casual conversation with one girl. Be genuinely interested in finding out where she's coming from and what her passions are. Make her laugh as often as possible. And by the end of the conversation, get a drink napkin, tear it in half, write your name and number in front of her on one half. Then hand her the other blank half of the napkin and a pen and wait until she figures out what to do with it. After she writes her name and number, then you 'trade' her your number for hers. I promise you, if you had a good conversation with the girl and she's single, 99% of the time she'll write her name and number on the other half of the napkin."

"I bet you're right," I said.

"Yeah, that's how I first met the mother of these guys." He pointed to the kids in the pool. "Do you see how this ties back to your interview approach? Instead of calling every employer you come across and begging for the job, you need to change your approach and prove to them that you're different; that you know what it means to understand *their* perspective about hiring you. You need to use a sniper rifle instead of a shotgun. What many people don't realize is that it's not just how many interviews you go on but also your interviewing skills that determine your likelihood of being successful with landing more interviews or getting hired."

"Makes sense to me," I said. "So, in the past, my interviewing tactics were using the shotgun approach. I've been trying to get my name OUT there to the employer?"

"That's where the misconception forms, Adrian. That's where, in my opinion, our school system, many of the so-called advisers in the career center, whoever has been teaching you how to get a job, have failed you."

"Right... I know that college isn't teaching me what I need to know. That's part of the reason I've been so upset lately. I felt like I tried so hard to get good grades in school and trusted that the educational system would take care of me, at least in getting hired after college. But now I realize that my education has done practically nothing to get me a job in the real world."

"People are years behind in their tactics for getting jobs and training people to get jobs. Newly hired employees at all sorts of companies have spent four years and hundreds of thousands of dollars on Ivy League educations, and as soon as they get a job, someone has to retrain them. School has given them the wrong attitude; it has instilled outdated systems of self-marketing, and it has done little to teach you what successful job hunting means in the real world."

"I think I'm just now starting to realize that. It's brutal out there. I'm nervous that I won't be able to find *anything*. And as much as I hate thinking about going back to school, I might get my MBA to buy me more time until the economy starts turning around."

"You could do that..." He paused and tilted his head. "But if you want my honest opinion, Adrian, I got my MBA, and it hasn't done a damn thing for me. Don't get me wrong, you'll be able to get a decent-paying job... maybe even at a *Fortune 500* company somewhere. But other than that, there's not much an MBA offers that you can actually use in the real world." The kids wrestled one another off the end of the diving board. Robert cringed, covered his eyes, and shook his head. "If you want some helpful advice from someone who's been in the trenches, I'd suggest saving your money and focusing on getting some real-world work experience instead of going further into debt. Most people think that by getting their MBA they will automatically become successful. This is backwards. I became successful first and then I went back to school and got my MBA. But like I said, that's only my partial perspective; you can try it on like a hat, and if it fits, you can use it. If not, throw it away."

Emily had warned me against the MBA idea, and now I'd heard it from the horse's mouth. I felt uneasy knowing that what I had learned from the authority figures in school was not what leads a person to success. I'd been looking up to and listening to the wrong people for so long...

"Anyway, we're on a tangent. Are you following me on what we've talked about so far?"

"I think I'm starting to understand what you mean by 'getting their perspective in here.'"

"And that is..." he said, rolling his hand for me to continue.

"I've got to start thinking like the employer. I can't go into an interview begging for a job. I've got to have my ducks in a row and know WHO they want and WHY. I spent so much time just tossing around applications, trying to get my NAME noticed, when I should have been stepping back and looking at the process from their eyes."

"That's right," he said. "See, there are two mindsets when it comes to the hiring process: that of the hiring manager and that of the job seeker. These perspectives are complete opposites. The mindset of the hiring manager is to get the most work out of an employee while spending the least amount of money. The mindset of the average job seeker is to find the highest-paying job that requires the least amount of work. Your goal as an 'enlightened' job seeker is not to fit into the category of the latter. Having an entitled mindset of 'I should get paid lots of money for the least amount of effort because I'm worth it' will guarantee you unemployment or job misery. You need to understand what the hiring manager is looking for in an employee, while also making sure you're getting a fair deal. It's all about understanding what they want and what you want. From there you will find a happy medium."

"I never thought about the dual-mindset of the hiring process, but it's *so* true."

"You bet it is. One of the biggest fears of employers is mis-hiring someone. A candidate may appear qualified at first glance; however, all too often, employees cannot deliver as promised and are terminated. Thus, the employer must begin the hiring process again. With the amount of time it takes to post the job opening, interview candidates, make a decision, and train the best candidate, a firm could lose exorbitant amounts of money."

"How much money?" I was curious.

"Well according to the book *TopGrading* by Brad Smart, the company could lose 10 to 12 times the employee's annual salary."

"Damn!" I said.

"Yeah, it's no joke. Think about it like this: If a company mis-hired a person who makes $35,000, it could eventually cost the employer between $350,000 and $420,000 to deal with the problems and fix the situation."

"That's a ton of money. No wonder it's extremely important for employers to hire the right candidate from the get-go."

"You got it."

He pulled out his iPhone and called up a search window. He typed something and I waited. "Take a look at these two book titles and tell me which one sold more copies."

I looked at the screen. One of the books was titled *Controlling Your Weight: The Thinking Consumer's Guide to Weight Control*. I had to read it a second time, and even then I didn't totally understand it. The second book was titled *Skinny Bitch*. I laughed out loud.

"*Skinny Bitch*?" I said.

"You're right... but why?"

"It's shorter, more to the point..."

"Yeah. That's right. But that's not the only reason. It's because the guy who wrote the first one had a fancy doctorate degree and thought of their audience as a university professor grading a paper. The person who wrote the second book was an ex-model. She thought from the mind of the CONSUMER. 'What would I have bought back when I was trying to lose weight?' she asked herself. And that is how she titled a winner."

"I see."

"So, next time you're going for an interview, remember to put yourself in the shoes of your employer. Instead of thinking by the books, try to think like the business you're applying for. Ask yourself these questions: One: Who is my prospective employer and interviewer? Two: What problems and frustrations are they facing? How can I alleviate those? Three: What is the result or outcome that our prospective employer wants to achieve? And, furthermore, how can YOU help them achieve it?"

I agreed with him. It made total sense.

He continued, "We have to realize that words have power. When you're writing your life accomplishments on your résumé, you've got to make it count. Every word, every detail, everything counts. I mean, what sounds better to you: 'Cleaned up client database,' or 'Helped retain $1.2 million by working 55-hour weeks for six weeks to clean up database for firm's newest client in 2006?'"

"The second one. Emily touched on this with me, and we made some changes to my résumé, but now I'm really starting to get the picture."

"Good."

"You know, it's taken me 23 years to learn most of this stuff. Twenty-three years."

"That's a long time."

"It is. It's a really long time, and even now I'm still learning. Although, had I sought help earlier in my life, it would have never taken me that long. As they say: You live and you learn… You, on the other hand, are learning from the mistakes of others early while you're still young. You're in a good position to succeed."

"Thanks to you and Emily. I really appreciate it—a lot."

"I know you do. I can tell." He watched the kids splashing in the water. "Alright, ready for the last lesson?"

"Sure. Let's hear it," I said.

"Years ago I worked with a client that taught me about the factors of success. She had told me about a study held at some university of the top salespeople who made over $240K a year in sales. They were looking for all the factors these salespeople had in common. Of all the different factors and research done, they found there was only one factor that was the key to being successful: Speed of Execution."

"What's Speed of Execution?" I asked.

"Glad you asked… It's the distance between the time that you hear something and you learn something, and the time you put it into action."

"Right. Once these salespeople got an idea, they implemented it immediately. They didn't sit around and think about it and wait to ask seven of their friends who aren't that successful what they thought of it. They just did it and implemented it. So, when you go home tonight and tomorrow, instead of sitting around contemplating what we've discussed today and waiting for the 'right time' to implement what you've learned, just go ahead and get it done. You'll be that much closer to your goal."

"That makes sense," I said. "People don't act on what they've learned. I feel like most of us know a lot and are well educated, but do very little to turn our thoughts into a reality."

"You got that right."

After several more minutes we parted ways. I drove home in a silent car. No music. Just the wind pushing against me as I sped toward my house. I walked through the door and found the place hadn't changed very much since I left it yesterday evening. I climbed the stairs and opened my laptop. I opened the folder containing my résumé and set to work. I would implement the changes IMMEDIATELY. In fact, from now on, I would do everything at the speed of light. I could feel a change in the way I had been looking at the world. I started to see the matrix.

I had two interviews coming up this week. I needed to start implementing my new knowledge in my interview practices. I knew Potter & Sons and Farnam Partners were both excellent firms, but my desire to work for them was not as strong as it was for Empyrean. These companies were merely stepping stones leading me to Empyrean. Despite the fact that I didn't want to work for either of them, I could not afford to screw up the interviews. I needed to give it everything I had in order to measure my skills against the competition.

I took Emily's advice about clear visions creating causes and began telling myself I was going to ace these interviews. These companies had no idea what was coming their way. It was time to take my job-hunting skills to the next level, time to pool my resources and design a strategy in which employers came to me.

It was time for a change.

NO ONE IS BETTER THAN YOU,
BUT YOU ARE NO BETTER
THAN ANYONE ELSE UNTIL
YOU DO SOMETHING TO PROVE IT.

· ·

—DONALD LAIRD, PH.D.
Author of *The Psychology of Selecting Employees*

CHAPTER 4

DEMONSTRATING VALUE

E mily had recently returned home from her vacation, and I was discussing my previous interviews with her. She seemed to think that I was on the right track but that I still had a ways to go.

I had achieved mild success with improving my speed of execution. I felt like things were moving faster in my life, propelling me toward some sort of prosperous end. My interviews with Farnam Partners and Potter & Sons had gone relatively well. Both companies were fairly small start-ups, and I wasn't super impressed with where the leaders had taken their businesses.

Farnam Partners operated out of some guy's home office, which I was a little put off by since I was used to working in an office building at my previous internship. Potter & Sons' office, though not in a house, was located in a rough part of town. Although they attempted to be professional by having office equipment like a copy machine and individual workstations, there was something amiss with the operation. The people were really friendly and social. In fact, they might've been a little bit too social. I judged this from the half-empty box of Bud Lights turned over on its side in the corner of the interview room.

Regardless of how prepared or professional my interviewers were, I felt pretty good about my performance.

Several days later, Emily and I met at the coffee shop to discuss my meeting with Robert.

"So how'd it go with Robert? You learn something?"

"Yeah, you were right; he really knows his stuff."

"You send him a follow-up email?"

I stared at her blankly. "What? No, what do you mean? I've been up to the charity twice this week to volunteer. I didn't think I needed to send him an email."

"Did you see him there?"

"No."

"In that case, you should have sent him a thank you card or a little gift telling him that you appreciated his help. It's good business etiquette, especially since he spent an entire afternoon teaching you."

"You're right, but it's already been a week. Do you think I should still send him something?"

"Of course you should. Why wouldn't you?"

I couldn't think of a reason not to. "I'll email him this afternoon then," I said.

"Did you send a follow-up letter to Potter & Sons? And what was the other company you interviewed at?"

"Farnam Partners."

"Right, did you send a follow-up letter to both companies after your interview?"

I felt a sinking feeling in the pit of my stomach. "No, was I supposed to?"

Emily covered her face with her hands and took a deep breath. She let out a long sigh through her palms. "Come on Adrian, you need to follow-up in ALL forms of business interactions—*especially* after a job interview. The more you communicate with employers, the more likely they will be to remember you, and the better your chances of getting ahead."

We continued to talk and she drove us home. I went into my room and sent Robert West an email. My phone rang: Jake.

"Hey man," I said.

"Hey, you wanna go to the library?" he asked. "I've got tons of work going on and I need somebody to talk to. It's driving me insane trying to do all of this in my bedroom."

"Yeah, that sounds good. I'll meet you there in 15."

"You eat yet?"

"No."

"I'll bring some lunch up there. Sit in the computer lab in the far corner; that way the lady can't see us while we eat."

The library was more important than these follow-up letters. I searched on Google and had a generic one copied in less than two minutes. I pasted the company names over the previous ones, sent two separate emails, and bolted out the door.

I arrived at the library and walked up the staircase toward the computer lab. The sign hung above the door: "NO Food or Drinks in Computer

Lab!" I laughed and found two free spaces in the corner. Jake was always late, so I knew I had time to kill. I put on my iPod and started playing solitaire on the computer. Several signs clearly stated "Computers are for academic use only."

I looked out through the bunker-like windows and wondered why, if they didn't want people to eat in the computer lab, they would wall it off and build tiny, somewhat tinted windows as the only way to see inside.

A good song came on and I turned up the volume. Seeing as how I was in the far corner, I felt it was OK to hum along with the music.

"Damn," I said to myself. I saw a girl walk by the windows. She looked good... damn, in fact, she looked *really* good. I couldn't quite make out her face, but she was headed my way. I leaned up to see a bit more clearly through the windows.

"Shit!" I whispered. It was Isabelle. And damn it, I had never responded to her text... She was headed right for me. I crouched behind my computer and signed into my email; this way I would look busy if she walked into the room.

I didn't look up from the screen, and fortunately she breezed by the lab without seeing me. My email took several more seconds to load. Robert had responded already. The guy charged $20k a day for his services and yet he still found time to respond to my mail. Incredible.

I opened the file and read:

Hey Adrian,
I had a good time on Saturday. Thanks for taking care of the kids... they seemed to enjoy your company.

Say, do you remember what I told you about my client telling me about the speed of implementation? Well, I'd forgotten to mention that she just so happens to be one of the BEST salespeople I know... and trust me; I know tons of salespeople.

Anyway, she's going to be in town this weekend, speaking at a training seminar for a group of high-level sales professionals. She gave me two free passes to go see her present on stage, but I promised my parents I'd bring the kids to go see them this weekend so I won't be able to make it to the seminar. Besides, I've already seen her on stage and she's a riot. (Normal admission for the seminar is $2000 at the door.) If you're interested, I could set you up *with my tickets and arrange a meeting between the two of you after her presentation... It's up to you.*

Her name is Tammy Turner. Ask Emily about her if you need more info.

-Robert

P.S. And don't forget to implement what we talked about last week! Get THEIR perspective in HERE!

I sat there and tried to figure it out. I tried to apply the information to my life. What could I do to make myself more marketable? More knowledgeable? I couldn't figure it out. I looked around the library, pondering my next moves.

The girl at the computer beside me was ordering a book on Amazon.com. I sat up straighter, squinted at her screen, and typed www.amazon.com into the browser. The website came up and I began searching for books. I needed something, a guide on how to make my interviewing campaign a success.

Jake arrived, slinging his bag beneath the table and handing me a sandwich.

"Thanks," I said.

I continued to skim the titles, searching for anything that would help me get the employer's perspective *in here*. I eventually settled on two books with the best reviews. Why settle for second best, right? I added the two books to my shopping cart: *TopGrading* and *Hire with Your Head*. I stared at the order confirmation and smiled. This would work. In addition to getting all the secrets from Emily and Robert, I would come at this problem with research of my own. It would make me that much more ready to take on the corporate world.

"You ready for spring break?" Jake asked.

"Hell yeah," I said. "I can't wait to have a week off. I'll be able to get a little R&R and maybe even some of my job-hunting stuff taken care of."

"For sure."

The librarian walked past and I held a bite in my mouth and didn't chew. She smiled at me, my half-eaten sandwich concealed beneath the partition behind the computer. I smiled, closed mouth, and nodded.

That afternoon, after the library fizzled out into pure boredom of Jake trying to friend girls he'd never even met on Facebook, I went home and found Emily at work in the kitchen. She was preparing a meal for Josh and his family at our place and was then planning to drive it over to his folk's house in Marietta County.

"How's it going?" I asked. "Whatcha making?"

"It's Indian," she smiled. "And it's healthy. I don't think you'd like it very much."

"I've got good taste," I defended. "It's just that I can't afford to expand upon it."

We laughed. She stuck a ladle in front of my face and I tasted the sauce. It was strong, almost too strong, and I squinted and backed away.

"Too spicy?"

"No," I said. "Not at all." I went into fridge and took out the milk. My parents had spotted me another $200 loan. It wasn't much, especially to some of the kids that went to this college, but it could hold me until things got better.

"I got an email back from Robert West."

"And?"

"You ever heard of Tammy Turner?" I asked.

"YEAH!"

I almost dropped my glass she yelled so loud.

"I LOVE Tammy Turner," Emily said. "She's a great writer."

"Yeah, well, I got some free tickets to her seminar this weekend. I'm not really sure I want to go."

"What are you talking about?"

"Well, I just figured that since I'm more interested in marketing than sales that I should—"

"Adrian... Jeez..." she shook her head in disbelief. "Marketing skills will get you in the door. Being able to sell yourself during the interview will get you the job."

I paused for a moment and contemplated what she told me. "Shoot," I said, shaking my head. "I hadn't thought of it like that. So, I guess the sales thing is important, isn't it?"

"Yeah, it is. Really important. And Tammy is awesome to hear. You know those tickets to her seminar aren't cheap, either."

"Yeah..."

"They're probably in the neighborhood of $2,000."

"Yeah, that's what Robert said in his email."

"I've been practicing improving my speed of execution," I said. "From now on, whenever I think of something that needs to be done, instead of writing it down or putting it off until later, I just do it."

"That's a huge step in being successful. Did Robert tell you to do that?"

"Yeah."

"He's a smart guy, isn't he?"

"Yeah, he really is."

She picked up several pots, covered them, and I helped her load them into the trunk of her car. "I'm glad you hadn't already given those tickets away. Hearing Tammy speak on sales is arguably just as important as learning from Robert, especially if you want to be able to consistently CLOSE the deal and get your employers to take out their wallets... which is, after all, what you want to do."

"Well, I've got two tickets. Would you like to come?"

"Of course I want to come! That would be awesome." She gave me a hug.

"Have fun at dinner," I said.

I watched from the driveway as her car disappeared down the road. There was a moment of peace on the front porch, the empty street echoing with the sound of her exhaust. The trees swished easily with the wind and I sighed, thinking for a long moment about all that lay before me.

PART TWO

It was the night of the seminar. Emily stood outside of my car, checking her hair in the passenger side window.

"Let's roll," I said. "We don't have all night!"

She laughed at me and got inside. "My hair is acting funny," she said. "I just have to make sure it looks perfect tonight."

"Well, it's taken you long enough..."

I sped off toward the Hilton hotel, toward Tammy Turner, toward more knowledge and insight. I felt great all of a sudden, like I'd really been let into a secret inner-circle of people who made more of themselves than the bare minimum.

Emily pointed through the window of the vehicle. I followed her finger, looking up at the hotel glowing brightly in the night sky. I hadn't been to this part of town in months. Why would a broke college kid like me ever have a reason to cruise the financial district?

We pulled to a stop beneath a large overhang. I stepped out of the car and handed the red-vested valet a $1 bill. It was the only cash I had in my wallet. I looked at the doorway and a feeling of sheer nervousness crept into my stomach. I took a deep breath and pushed it away.

We walked into the building, surveying the crowd of middle-aged business people drinking from tall crystal flutes of wine or champagne. We showed our tickets to a hulking man in a tuxedo shirt at the doorway. He smiled kindly and led us inside. An older gentleman put a nametag around our necks and led us to our tables. We were in the back of a golden ball-room, beneath a lavish archway, watching as the entire hotel buzzed with conversation and life.

"No one told me this was such a big deal," I said, noticing some of the tables occupied by leaders of major companies. Robert sure had his hands deep in the financial soil of this city. Seats like these were worth a fortune.

The crowd hushed and a middle-aged man took the stand. "Ladies and gentlemen, we've got a special speaker tonight..." He gave a brief but glowing introduction. "I'm proud to introduce Tammy Turner!" he said, stepping down from the stage. The crowd erupted with applause, immediately standing and holding their hands high in the air. Tammy walked gingerly across the stage, waving at the audience.

I could tell right away that there was something special about her, something that made her words so valuable to all of these people. I looked at Emily and studied her expectant expression. She was engrossed in the woman's presence before the first word had been uttered. The applause continued, and Tammy nodded gratefully at the crowd.

Tammy spoke, "You know, most of the time when I ask a salesperson how they fair at public speaking, they typically respond, 'Eh, it's not my strongest attribute.'

"I always find this interesting because, as a salesperson, you spend the majority of your time speaking to prospects in an effort to make a good impression and gain their trust. Whether you're at home, at work, or in your car, 80% of your day is spent communicating verbally. People are deciding whether or not they like you within a very short period of time."

Tammy moved around the stage, stepping carefully across the black polished floor and making eye contact with nearly everyone in the room. Her poses were casual, yet refined and tasteful. She exploded every sentence like a gunshot but remained constantly in control of her voice. "People determine if they like you based on the *way* that you speak and present yourself. For example, a woman will typically determine whether or not she likes you in about 15 seconds." The crowd chuckled, sensing a joke. "Have any of you gentlemen ever dated one of these types of women?" The male audience members gave a warm rustle of appreciation. "You see," she continued, "men are a little more generous. They give you 35 to 40 seconds before they decide whether or not they like you."

She nodded her head, as though she were formulating something. "So, what are we saying here?" She raised her arms in question. "Well, we're saying men are slower..." The audience greeted this with a ROAR of laughter and applause. She grinned and waved for the room to be quiet, as though the joke had been an accident, a secret, something that should've remained for women only. We were only 60 seconds into the presentation, and already Tammy Turner owned the room.

"No, I'm just teasing... But, in all seriousness, folks, anytime that you make a cold call, you've got approximately 37 seconds to make an impression... 37 seconds isn't a heck of a lot of time. Now, let's say you've got a face-to-face presentation with Mr. Smith, the COO of a *Fortune* 500 company. You've got a maximum of about 5.3 minutes to make an impression. That's not a whole lot of time either."

Everyone nodded in agreement. People remained fixed on Tammy's glowing aura.

"We have differences in the way we speak, the way we communicate, the way we present ourselves. And what does all of this tell us? It tells us, unfortunately, that the majority of the time, people are determining whether or not they like us, and initially, it has absolutely nothing to do with your professional knowledge."

Everyone agreed.

"So, before I go any further, let me see a quick show of hands. How many of you have ever had the privilege of having one of your sales presentations videotaped and actually WATCHED it? Anybody?" Most people in the audience raised their hands, including Emily. She'd never told me this… "GOOD! And how many of you find that to be a feel-good, happy experience?" The audience sensed Tammy's sarcasm, and laughter echoed throughout the ballroom.

"Most people say they'd rather get their nails removed with pliers than see their sales pitch for a second time."

I looked over at Emily. Her laptop was open on the table. She was typing. During a rush of laughter I asked her about it. "You brought your laptop with you?"

"Heck yeah! I'm a slow writer and I wanna make sure I don't miss anything."

Tammy Turner went on to discuss the ins and outs of analyzing your sales pitches, demonstrating value, making sure that your persuasive skills are up to par. Her tactics for Demonstrating High Value especially caught my attention. I wish she had elaborated a bit more on that… Maybe I'd get a chance to ask Emily for an explanation after things died down.

Following the action-packed hour-long speech, there was a brief ten-minute bathroom break before dinner was served. Everyone got out of their seats and stretched. All of a sudden I felt something tugging on the back of suit jacket.

"What the—" I turned around and saw Emily crouched behind me.

"What are you doing?"

"Hiding," she said abruptly.

"I see that, but *who* are you hiding from?" I was getting impatient. I could tell Emily didn't want to tell me. There was a group of seemingly high-level executives staring at us wondering what in the hell had gotten into this girl.

"Stop it!" I whispered loudly. "You're making a scene. What has gotten into you?"

She finally let out a sigh, and said, "Remember when I was telling you about that guy I slept with? The one before I met Josh? Well, the guy is standing right over there." She pointed over my shoulder.

My head made it about halfway until she grabbed the lapel on my suit jacket and yanked my attention back to her.

"Don't look now!"

"Hey watch it! You're putting wrinkles in my suit."

"Don't be so obvious then!"

"Fine…" I slowly turned my body around, pretending to look at the lavishly decorated ballroom. When I finally made my way around to lock my eyes on Emily's mystery lay, that's when I felt my heart stop.

"You've got to be kidding me, Emily."

"What?"

"Oh my God… It's the really young guy with the brown hair? Red tie? Talking to the old guy with the wine glass?"

She peeked out, "Yes, yes, yes… that's him. Don't tell me you actually *know* him…" Emily was getting anxious. I couldn't respond. I couldn't move. It was as though my body went into shock. I blushed, an expression of sheer panic flooding my face like molten lava.

"Adrian!" Emily yelled, trying to snap me out of my coma. All I could do was repeat his name—like a broken record player in my head: "Kyle Calloway… Kyle-Fucking-Calloway…"

PART THREE

"Emily Anderson and Adrian Addler?"

We were approached by an usher. It broke me out of my trance so hard you'd have thought I was wearing an electric dog collar.

"Yes?" we chimed in unison, Emily still concealed behind me.

"Ms. Turner is expecting you. She has made arrangements for you to meet her for dinner, compliments of Robert West."

We looked at each other in disbelief and followed the man as he stepped gingerly through the maze of tables and chairs. Tammy instantly remembered Emily from the last time she had done a speech. They smiled, shook hands, and Emily introduced me as well.

"So, you're Adrian Addler? The one Robert told me about."

"That's right," I said.

We spoke for a few minutes as the crowd settled down and prepared for dinner to be served. Robert had pre-ordered the dishes the day before. Emily, who seemed to have calmed down by this point, was having the Chilean sea bass and I was having the Wanchese Bay jumbo diver scallops.

Tammy was speaking to someone else, and I took a moment to scold Emily.

"I can't believe you slept with that asshole!" I whispered. "He's two years younger than you... and he's a jackass."

"Why do you hate him so much? I've never heard you talk about him before."

"Well, I guess I didn't hate him... that much... until now... Why did you hook up with him?"

"He lied and told me that he was my age. He seemed mature enough, so I went with it."

"What a shithead... what a—"

"Shh," Emily said, fake smiling at me. "Keep it down or you'll get us busted." She laughed and patted me on the shoulder. We took our seats and ate. I had ample time to ask Tammy some questions about my current situation. I very suddenly realized that I didn't know where to begin.

She chuckled and started for me, "Don't you wish an employer would just come right out and TELL you what they want? Wouldn't that make it so much easier?"

"Yeah, sure," I said.

"Well, sadly, that's not the way it happens. But, what I can tell you is this: Employers want 'A-Players.' An A-Player is someone who finds ways to get the job done in *less time* with *less cost.* The more value you're able to demonstrate as an A-Player, the more attractive you'll look as a candidate. The trick is demonstrating that YOU have higher value than your competition."

"Demonstrating Value..." I tried to formulate a response.

She spoke too quickly. "Your goal going into an interview is to stand out from the crowd."

"Just like when we made your résumé and cover letter attractive by using some marketing tactics," Emily said.

I nodded and looked back at Tammy.

"That's exactly right. You want to add the same type of 'marketing tactics' to your personal interview by giving answers that Demonstrate Value. You need to be specific, prepared, confident, but at the same time you must avoid being arrogant or cocky. Don't come off as a know-it-all. Come off as an intelligent person who can get the job done."

"That makes sense, but how do I Demonstrate Value if I'm just being quizzed on past abilities?" I asked.

"Good question," Tammy said. "You Demonstrate Value by telling stories."

"Stories?" I said, unsure if I heard her correctly.

"That's right, you tell your interviewer a success story. In some of the cutting-edge research that I've done on human psychology, I've discovered that our minds actually only understand things in relationship to a *story.*" Tammy nodded, really stressing this point. "When a prospective employer is looking at your résumé or listening to your answers during the interview, their radar is in full effect; they're very sensitive to what you say, and they're listening for the memorable details. What they're doing is going through a process of being very critical. They're trying to decide whether or not you're very credible, whether or not they can trust you, and ultimately whether or not they like you...

"All of these things are happening because of their critical minds. And, as it turns out, one of the things that successful marketers, salesmen, and psychologists have discovered is that *stories* cut through all of the skepticism, suspicion, and psychological defense mechanisms that people have when they don't know you. Stories go right past the critical mind."

"That's some pretty cool stuff," Emily said. "I think you touched on that in your last book, only it had to do with selling and how people are essentially absorbed in what you have to say without giving a lot of resistance."

"That's right, Emily—good memory," Tammy said approvingly. "And by intentionally emphasizing the elements of your work experience that are very compelling, you design a story that helps a prospective employer get to know you, relate to you, build trust with you, and that also frames you in the right light. This can be very, very powerful in helping you demonstrate your value and dramatically increasing your chances of getting the job offer."

"So when would I want to tell a story during the interview?" I asked. This was starting to sound like a lot of work. I could barely get my answers straight, let alone tell a story about my previous work experience.

"Another good question, Adrian. If I'm in an interview and an employer asks me a question like, 'Can you tell me a little about yourself?' I would not be doing myself any favors by stating general facts or answers. Lofty claims like 'I am a hard worker' or 'I am self motivated' will get the employer to raise their flag of suspicion. Statements like these are unsubstantiated. Instead, the way I would approach this question would be to tell a story about how I started my own landscaping business with a crew of four during the summer quarter of my sophomore year while simultaneously taking on a full school load."

"Wow, is that true?" I asked.

"It sure is. Times were tough back then. But, do you see how one of your answers could be much more compelling when it is encapsulated in a story? It just becomes so much more powerful."

"Yeah, totally." I nodded my head in amazement. I couldn't believe what I was hearing.

Someone tapped on Tammy's shoulder and she turned away. It was the old man who had been speaking with Kyle a few minutes earlier. I saw Kyle standing behind him and immediately turned away. I looked for Emily, but she was already gone. It appeared that she was pacing around the room aimlessly. I watched as one of the waiters approached her and asked if everything was OK. She nodded and said something but kept walking.

"Adrian, where were we?"

"Om…" I looked back at Tammy. Kyle had been introduced for a brief greeting and was on the way back to his table, the old man leading the way.

"Let's start with SOIs," she said.

Before I had a chance to ask what SOI meant, she was already on a roll.

"You have to remember to gauge your actions according to what each individual employer responds to. You can do this via small indicators in their behavior. We call these Signs of Interest, or SOIs."

"Really?" I was in shock. I couldn't believe what I was hearing. There had actually been *signs* this whole time that I hadn't known about? I needed to probe deeper.

"Do you have any examples you could share?" My back straightened and I was sitting on the edge of my seat. Emily returned to the table, her head still somewhat turned away from Kyle's direction.

"Sure, there are a bunch, let me think… Perhaps the interviewer will lean toward you while you're speaking or give you compliments on some of your prior achievements. They might show genuine interest by asking lots of questions on how you carried out a project. Or maybe they'll talk about salary and benefits early on in the conversation before you've had a chance to fully demonstrate your value. The key here is to notice if they're exhibiting any approval-seeking behavior."

I recalled an incident I had with my last interviewer at Potter & Sons.

"So, if an employer compliments me on the way that I solved a problem during my internship and told me that the solution I came up with would be perfect for a similar problem that they presently have in their company, should take that as an SOI?"

"Of course. If they seem really interested, you're doing a good job. If the person seems bored, you should take that as an SOD, or Sign of Disinterest," she laughed. "In which case you would need to perk them up with a surprising experience that'll make you stand out. Talk about how you added a lot of value to your previous employer's business or come up with something witty that will make you stand out.

"Remember this rule of thumb: Communicate with impact or don't communicate at all. You can't bore the employer into wanting to hire you, just like you can't bore the opposite sex into feeling attracted to you. Speak their language enough so that they know you're on *their* page."

I remembered my P&P interview. Nothing about that guy had come close to the word "interested." I had gone as far as to call him a robot after listening to several pieces of my recorded interview. But, Robot or not, I could have still pushed his buttons and gotten a positive response.

My thoughts were shattered when she abruptly said, "So, Adrian, I heard that your last interview didn't go very well?"

"Well…" I was taken aback. Had Robert told her about this? How did she know? "I don't really know if it was good or bad."

"Did you record the interview?"

"Yes," I said, basking in my own righteousness.

"Do you have it with you?"

"No, it's at my house," I said, totally relieved.

"That's OK," Emily said, butting into the dialogue. "It's on my iPod."

My eyes widened to the size of boiled eggs. I watched as she fished around in her purse and passed the iPod across the table into the steady hands of Tammy Turner.

"It's OK Adrian," Tammy assured me. "I'll put one on my ear, you put one on yours, and we'll both listen at the same time. Only for a minute. No big deal." She looked at the small black device and pressed play. I shoved one of the white ear buds into the side of my head and waited.

The interview commenced:

Interviewer: I see… Can you please describe your ideal boss for me?

PAUSE

Tammy looked at me. "How did you answer this?"

"They were such loaded questions," I said. "I didn't know how to respond to something like that." I was trying to make excuses for my poor performance.

"But what did you say? Do you remember?"

I bit my lip in thought. "An ideal boss is one who never reprimands me, who always ups the salary, always has great ideas… I don't know."

PLAY

Adrian: I guess my ideal boss would be someone who respects me, sets realistic goals, doesn't micromanage, and doesn't keep changing his mind about deadlines every other day. And someone who is accessible when I have questions. I think that's key to a boss's performance: being able to answer questions.

Interviewer: What do you expect from this position?

Adrian: Uhhh... I don't know too much yet about the position. Only what the person doing the telephone interview mentioned to me. I'm very eager to hear more.

Interviewer: Sure. You'd be assisting the project team. You'd help the project manager stay organized, take care of all document organization, invoices, etc.

Adrian: Sounds very good.

Interviewer: What do you know about our company, Mr. Addler?

Adrian: I know that Proteus & Paulson has a reputation as a great place to work. That's why I sent in my résumé. You are my first choice.

Interviewer: Interesting. What are your strengths? Your outstanding qualities? What will you bring to P&P?

Adrian: People tell me I have excellent communication skills. That's one of my main attributes. I am also a people person, and I am a quick learner.

Interviewer: Alright... And what do you think is your greatest weakness?

Adrian: I'm a bit of a perfectionist sometimes... and so as a result I take longer to finish some projects because I want to make sure they're done right.

Interviewer: Well, that's not the worst BAD quality, is it?

Adrian: No, I guess not.

As I listened, it became apparent that I hadn't told them *any* stories during this interview. It's not that I didn't want to; I just didn't know how to before today. I had no idea that I was giving lofty claims during the interview. And now I could see that she was right; I really did sound like I was giving a bunch of jumbled, vague, generalized statements... I was doomed from the onset of the conversation.

"We can stop it now," I said to Tammy, nodding my head. "I realize what I did wrong."

"What's that?"

"I had no stories. I was too vague. I didn't paint myself in the best light. I thought I could just wing it and do well, but that obviously didn't work. I didn't give the employers what they wanted to hear."

"It's sometimes harder than it sounds. Employers fork out lots of money to fancy consultants who deliberately advise them not to tell you what they want. They're afraid that you'll mindlessly recite to them what they want to hear instead of revealing who you truly are in the moment, which is a logical argument if you think about it... but, it puts you, the interviewee, in a difficult position."

I recalled something from earlier and asked, "You mentioned that employers want A-Players. How do I show them that I'm an A-Player when I don't even know what an A-Player is?"

Tammy laughed at my string of questions. "It's fairly self explanatory, Adrian: An A-Player is a person who can be counted on to get the job done. A-Players will work 55 hours a week or more. They are intrinsically motivated to succeed. Obviously, not all employees are A-Players. The average employee, on the other hand, will work 40 to 49 hours a week. They are not nearly as motivated. An A-Player's motivation has no bounds. They find ways over, under, around, and through barriers, and frequently do so without asking for help. They desire success like others desire food, relaxation, or even rest."

"Right," I said. I knew I had what it took to become an A-Player. In fact, I had been an A-Player at my internship. My bosses could testify to that. Now, all I had to do was prove this to my potential employers...

Then I began to wonder, "What exactly are the values that I should demonstrate? I know that I'm supposed to show the employer how I can save them time and money, but what else is there?"

"There are many attributes of an A-Player. I mentioned a few earlier, but let me give you the real deal…" She paused, sipping her wine and looking up into the sparkling cathedral ceiling. "Alright, since we don't have all night to talk about this, let me explain the three most important attributes of an A-Player as it applies to the interview: psychological mindset, listening skills, and story-telling skills.

"The first is mindset. Believe it or not, this is one of the biggest factors." She took another sip, drained the glass. "Sorry, sometimes I need to relax after a week of speaking."

"I totally agree," I said. I took a sip of my beer, eager for her to drink as much as she wanted.

"Alright, psychological mindset…" she said, as though she had just figured out a way to explain this to me. "I met Michael Marks when I was skiing in Whistler Blackcomb."

"Michael Marks? The Olympic downhill champion?" Emily asked.

"Yeah, that's right. My husband and I were on the lift with him. Jerry, my husband, asked him, 'What was the trick to winning all those gold medals?' and Michael said, 'By the time you get to the medal rounds, every competitor is capable of running the fastest time. It's not a question of skill so much as a question of who can pull it off in a clutch situation, when the heat is really on, when the pressure is really on, and with the greatest consistency.' That's what I mean by psychological mindset."

"Wow," I said.

"So, it's really not how different you are from the other applicants, although that does count; it's how you're able to handle yourself when the rubber meets the road."

"Right." I'd never heard anyone say that before.

"The other huge thing you have to remember is that being a good listener is extremely important. Have you ever heard the saying, 'lead with your ears'?"

"I don't think so."

"Well, be sure to remember this: Leading with your ears is extremely important. A guy named Neil Rackham wrote a book called *SPIN Selling*. He had studied over 35,000 sales calls trying to figure out what makes a successful sale, and you know what he found out?"

I shook my head. The waiter set a full bottle of wine on ice in the center of the table. I pretended not to notice when Tammy poured another glass.

"He found out that the more you ask questions, the more successful the sales interaction is likely to be, especially if you ask the RIGHT questions. The same thing holds true for your job interviews, only instead of SPIN Selling, I gave this process a fancy name called *Extracting Values*."

"What does it mean?"

"Extracting Values refers to the process of drawing out information through conversation. You surmise what is important to your interviewer, usually with the intention of reaching a deep inner desire that motivates them in the first place. In terms of interviewing, Extracting Values may help a candidate determine that an employer who says they are *looking for a self-motivated individual* is really looking for someone who will *take ownership of a project and drive it to completion without asking to have his hand held or making up excuses*."

"Right."

"To do all of this stuff, you have to go into an interview prepared. Don't try to wing it like you did at..." She pointed at the iPod.

"Proteus & Paulson," I said.

"Right, don't ever wing it like that again."

"I won't."

"I've got a good example of Extracting Values." She took another sip on the wine and leaned forward in her chair. "I was at Nordstrom's looking for a dress to wear in a photo shoot for my website, and I was walking around, aimlessly looking for something in a size 8. A woman comes up to me and asks what I need. I said, 'Something in a size 8,' and she said, 'Hold on,' and walked away to help someone else."

I nodded that I was paying attention. The waiter set another beer down beside me. Good thing Robert West had pre-paid our dinner and drink bill...

"So, a few moments later, another salesperson came up to me and asked the same thing. I said the same thing, 'I'm looking for something in size 8,' and this one stopped, cocked her head quizzically, studied my body, and asked, 'What's the occasion?'"

"I see..." I said while nodding my head as if I understood. In reality, I didn't "see" at all. I do that sometimes in class, where I'll say I understand, even though I don't completely, just so the professor will keep on teaching. I figured the tactic would work here as well.

"Right, she was Extracting Values." Tammy cleared her throat. "So, I told her the occasion: a photo shoot for my website. She says, 'What kind of lighting? Describe the mood you're going for, this way I can help you look your best.'

"So, I describe what we were doing and she asked me if the dress is something I'll want to wear more than once or will I give it away after I'm through with it? Then she looked at me and said, 'Keep thinking about it, look around at the 8's that are right over there, and I'll be back to help you in two minutes.'

"And you know what? The other girl came back, pointed me in the direction of some other styles, and I told her that I was already being helped."

"Makes sense," I said. "You don't want to have a second-rate person helping you make a first-rate decision."

We sat quietly for several moments, each of us working at the drinks. Emily and Tammy made conversation about something unrelated to interviewing and I went to the men's room. I watched myself in the mirror as I washed my hands. The other guys in there were much older, red wine staining their lips, gold watches clasped to their wrists... perhaps one day I would have that kind of security.

I returned to the table. Tammy continued where she left off. "Are you ready for the last attribute of an A-Player?"

I looked at her with a confused expression. "I thought you said the last attribute was story-telling skills? Didn't we already cover that?"

"Yes, but I didn't tell you *how* to create your value-demonstrating stories. To successfully do that, you'll need to learn my secret formula that I've never told *anyone* else."

PART FOUR

T ammy leaned in close to Emily and me. She looked to her right and left in a confidential, 'just-between-you-and-me' pose.

"I've used this technique throughout my entire sales career, even before starting my own consulting business."

"And you've never told anybody?" Emily asked.

"Nope, and you can't tell anyone, either. And I mean that. Don't go ruining my secrets," Tammy laughed. "I keep this a secret because it's what puts me over the edge. It separates me from the competition, even though I own my own consulting business now, and I don't interview for jobs very often. And by 'very often,' I mean 'ever.' But, business owners never know how long they'll be able to stay afloat in this kind of economy. Every day the recession market forces people like me back onto the job hunt."

We nodded.

"So, why are you going to tell us then? You know, if it's such a big secret?" I felt Emily's heal kick my shin. I looked at her, a disgusted expression on her face saying *why did you just say that!*

Luckily, Tammy just laughed at my question and continued, "Because you two are young and you're trying to make something of yourselves. Robert trusts you, and I think you could really use this advice. More than anything though, I hold the belief that in order for a person to become wealthy and successful, they must learn to create as much value as possible in every situation, whether they're paid for it or not."

"Cool," I said. I admired Tammy's attitude and positive outlook on life.

"So, remember what I said? Communicate with impact or don't communicate at all?"

We both nodded our heads.

"Well, I developed this technique while I was still a screenwriting major in college. It comes from the universally understood plot structure of a movie script: Hero + Setting + Obstacle + Climax + Ending = Movie. I developed it because I realized that my interview dialogue was extremely weak, and my answers were so disorganized that I was often rambling for much longer than it should have taken me to tell my success stories."

Tammy paused and looked at me as if to imply what she was about to say would apply to me most of all. "And remember this: Your stories have to be organized in order to have value. People tend to think that giving the right response to a question is as simple as giving the correct 'answer.' This is wrong. An answer isn't enough information for the employer to understand who YOU really are. You need to back up every answer, every statement, with a story. People are more interested in experiencing the stories than in summaries. Just look at how many billions of dollars are spent at the box office every year when the same people could've easily gotten the gist of what happened in a movie review."

"Right..." I started putting the pieces together in my head.

She continued, "You have to think like a storyteller, which is why I developed this simple formula for crafting your stories. I call it the S.C.A.R.F. Formula."

"This sounds good..." I said.

"It is. Just wait." Tammy took a breath and looked around for a second time. She spoke very quickly, but precisely. "S.C.A.R.F. is a way to organize your personal success stories so that they're memorable and compelling. Remember it like this:

"The 'S' stands for 'SETTING.' As in, 'when and where did this story occur? If you think back to the last time you saw a movie, there was always a scene that set the stage for the rest of the film. The 'C' stands for 'CHALLENGE.' As in, 'what specific problem were you faced with?' In movies, there is always a problem or obstacle that the hero is faced with overcoming. You should use numbers to describe who and what was involved and what would've happened if you failed. Remember, it is very important to explain what was at stake."

"Got it," I said.

"Go on," Emily said. We were like racehorses beating down the gate.

"The 'A' stands for 'ACTION.' As in, 'what specific action did you take to complete the task?' This is where films tend to focus for the majority of the movie. They bring the audience along as the hero overtakes the obstacle. Similarly, your focus should be in describing your actions, which will allow your interviewer to visualize your achievements.

"The 'R' stands for 'RESULT.' As in 'bottom line results.' What happened at the end of your movie? What was the end result of you vanquishing the obstacle? Remember to convey your return on investment

(ROI) value not only from your perspective, but from the employer's perspective as well.

"Finally, the 'F' stands for 'FEEDBACK.' Similar to how movie makers need to be in line with what the producers want, you need to make sure you're in line with what the employer wants. Ask the interviewer a question to see if you are on the right track or if they would like more examples."

"That's awesome," I said. "I wrote it down. Is that OK?"

"Yes, that's fine. Just don't show anyone, please? We've all got to have our trade secrets, you know?"

"Sure do," I said.

Tammy wanted to make her next point *very* clear, so she leaned in close.

"Your stories must contain all of these elements, or they will not be a success. Moviegoers want to be enticed by what they are watching, not disappointed. Likewise, employers want to hear an entire story. They don't want to be left guessing at the end."

Tammy's movie analogy was making so much sense. I was beginning to understand that a successful interview relies on one's own compelling storytelling.

She continued, "So, at the end of your interview, did you ask any questions?"

"Not after the one we just heard on the iPod," I said, totally embarrassed. Tammy shook her head. "You're so fired," she said jokingly. It was good to poke fun at my mistakes. It helped me to not take them so seriously.

"But on my last two interviews, I did ask some general questions that I pulled from Google after my Dad scolded me about not asking anything at Proteus."

"That's not bad, but I think we could do one better than that," Tammy said confidently.

"What would that be?" I asked.

"I call it the Maverick Follow-Up technique."

"That sounds kind of fancy. Did Sarah Palin come up with it?" Emily asked jokingly.

We all laughed.

"Not exactly—but to prove to your interviewer that you want to be a valued member of their staff, you have to get an idea of what their top players are like. This technique consists of three questions. The first is, 'Out of your current employees, who would you choose as the top performer in this position?' This allows them to look at their staff and decide who their A-, B-, and C-Players are."

I nodded my head again, remembering her lesson on A-Players.

"Once you have the name of the person, ask your interviewer about what traits make him or her stand out. By asking this question you are able to compare your traits to those of the company's A-Players. Listen carefully to the list of traits the employer rattles off. You may want to write them down; this way you can remember them later."

"That's a really good idea," I said. "I always try to take notes. That's one thing I'm good at."

"That's good," Tammy said. "Building off of your strengths is very important during this process."

"Yeah," Emily chimed in, wanting to get to the point. "What's the last question?"

"Lastly, ask your interviewer, 'What specific actions or behaviors make him or her so successful?' Asking this allows you to gauge how your actions and behaviors stack up next to those of someone who has experience in your field. If you can demonstrate that you have the potential to be an A-Player, then your chances of landing the job are much higher."

Someone called Tammy away from the table and we finished our drinks. She made the rounds as people finished eating and shook hands, posed for pictures, anything the crowd asked. Luckily, Kyle and his grandfather left early and Emily was able to relax.

The night continued very peacefully, with the three of us quietly conversing in the center of our own universe. At midnight, we said our goodbyes and left the Hilton.

I felt good about myself.

Then, just in the middle of my great drive home, I remembered Kyle Calloway. I kept getting images… horrible images that danced like smiling demons inside my head. I didn't want to bring it up again because I didn't want to embarrass her. I knew it had been a mistake on her part, but I still could not get over how sleazy Kyle was. This just gave me another reason to dislike the guy… as if I needed one.

The Kyle thing only bothered me for a few seconds, and soon I was over it. I drove with confidence and ease down the Boulevard, cruising well below the speed limit, in no real hurry to get home. It was a new kind of sensation that I hadn't felt before. For the first time I felt like I knew something that very few other people knew. And, well... I did.

As I rounded the corner onto my street, I felt something come over me. I had acquired so much knowledge over the past month. I needed to start implementing what I learned. After all, I had told myself that I was going to improve my Speed of Execution. I felt I was finally ready to shoot for a company toward the top of my list.

IWC was a well-known name in the city. The company had just as good a reputation as Empyrean. The only differences between the two companies were that IWC didn't get as many awards and recognitions, and it didn't have offices in nearly every major city across the country like Empyrean did.

I pulled into the garage and ran up to my room. I checked to make sure IWC was still accepting applications and was relieved to see that they were. I may not have been entirely ready to take on such a huge company, but something inside me told me that, with all of the information and help I had received, I would do just fine in the interview.

My résumé looked good, and I read over it for the thousandth time. I attached it to the email and set the timer to send it at 8 a.m. the following morning. I hesitated slightly before getting offline, but I shook off any doubts and climbed into bed. I had been feeling tired on my drive home, but something was keeping me awake. I got up, opened my internet browser, and started researching IWC.

These guys had no idea what was about to hit them.

AS I GROW OLDER, I PAY LESS
ATTENTION TO WHAT MEN
SAY. I JUST WATCH WHAT
THEY DO.

....

—ANDREW CARNEGIE
Second-Richest Man in History after John D. Rockefeller

CHAPTER 5

COMPLICATIONS

The fresh breath of spring fell across the quad. Jake and I exited the building shaking our heads.

"That was one hell of a final," Jake said.

"Tell me about it. I haven't had time to do anything all week but study."

Our conversation was interrupted by an obnoxious voice booming down the sidewalk. Jake looked at me and shook his head, "Here comes our beloved president and his insanely hot girlfriend." Jake nodded his head toward Kyle Calloway. "I don't know what she sees in that guy…"

"How's it going guys?" he said with an air of authority. He was dressed as if he had just come from a J. Crew magazine shoot. I contemplated asking what time his yacht set sail for the Hamptons and if he was planning on taking the sophomore sorority girl he was with the other day, but I couldn't bring myself to be a home wrecker.

"It's going alright," Jake said.

"You hear about Heather Greenstein?"

We shook our heads, trying to appear disinterested. I didn't want to hear more bad news. I was sick of bad news, yet people never got tired of spreading it. Ever since I found out that he had slept with Emily I couldn't look at him without a feeling of reserved hatred. Granted, I had very little respect for him to begin with, but after learning that little piece of information, any hope of burying the hatchet was completely lost.

"She got a 74 on the finance final. Can you believe it? Of all people, Heather Greenstein! She actually cried when she found out," he said.

Kyle was such a tool… I wanted to turn and walk away, but I couldn't work up the courage to be an asshole. I had to be the better man.

"So, I hear you're gunning for Empyrean?" he said, looking at me.

"Who told you that?"

He shrugged. "Word travels."

Kyle's girlfriend butted in, "Kyle, please..." she shoved him, "Adrian, *I* heard that you were applying to Empyrean from Sarah Martinez, who heard it from Emily Anderson."

So, Emily was giving up my information...

"It's more like I'm *thinking* about applying."

Kyle butted in again, even though I wasn't looking at him. "Either way, you've got some steep competition. I plan on applying. So do Chip and Delaney. All in all, I think about 30 of us are applying from our class alone."

"I guess I'll make 31." I imagined staring at him over a Wild West card table, my hand on my pistol and the other hand holding my cards. A near empty fifth of whiskey between us. Hot sweat on my forehead. Two pair in my hand, aces and deuces. The last card coming. It's an ace! I lay 'em down, reach for the pile of gold in the center of the table...

Kyle stands up, draws. My hand is faster. The Colt .45 hits him, one in the gut and one in the chest. He flies backward and raises his gun. He lets off a shot but it misses and the bottle of whiskey explodes on the table. The women are scattering throughout the barroom. The horses are neighing. I send another one at him. This one strikes him right between the eyes. I lay my cards down. Full house, Aces and Deuces. Bitch.

Then the dream ended. Kyle was still walking along with his girl-friend, his extremely hot girlfriend, and I was still walking with Jake.

"Thirty-one's a hell of a crowd to be applying for one position," Kyle said, wincing like he was tearing off a Band-Aid. It was his way of saying that he thought I wouldn't make the cut. He changed his tone and added, "Anyway, I just wanted to say good luck with the job, Addler."

"Good luck to you too, Calloway."

"See you later, Adrian," his girlfriend said, smiling and waving at me.

Kyle shook my hand and they disappeared into a crowd of bodies.

*   *   *

Upon my arrival at the apartment, I noticed that my books from Amazon were on the front porch. I shredded the packing material and set them on the counter. School was out for a full week. It meant that I could get my job search back on track.

I went into the library, which was a virtual ghost town, and took a seat at one of the computers in the far corner. It was my home now, a figurative den tucked away from the angry librarians and prying eyes. I took a few moments to think. What did I need to work on the most? I couldn't figure it out... Then I remembered one of the fundamentals: "Get THEIR perspective in HERE."

I needed to shed my *employee*-focused approach to getting hired and rewire myself to becoming *employer*-focused. In order to do this, I'd need to continually train myself to think like the employer I was aiming to be hired by.

I stayed in the library, which was rather nice when uninhabited, for an entire week of reading and information cramming. If I wasn't A-Player material, I don't know what is. I devoured my first book, *Hire with Your Head,* which taught me that many managers don't truly understand how to make good hiring decisions. They often choose prospective employees based on gut reactions, which I thought was interesting. The key to dodging this pitfall as the applicant would be to appeal to the employer's *reason* and *emotion.*

Next I tackled *Top Grading,* which I'd have to say was a beast of a book. I ended up just skimming through the chapters to learn about what happens to companies who end up mis-hiring their employees. Robert was right. It ends up costing companies who mis-hire employees 14.2 times the salary of that individual after you factor in all of the HR costs, recruiting costs, executive management, severance packages, etc.

After exhausting my own resources I went to the public library and checked out books on team building. One that really helped was Patrick Lenconi's *The Five Dysfunctions of a Team.* This book helped convey the idea that building a cohesive team translates into big bucks for a company. The challenge with this, however, is overcoming the human behavioral tendencies known to corrupt teams—i.e., absence of trust, fear of conflict, lack of commitment, avoidance of accountability, and inattention to results.

*   *   *

After completing the initial stint of library research, I decided to dive back into the job hunt and get to work on crafting my stories and touching up my résumé. I made my stories more vivid and commanding by using Tammy's S.C.A.R.F. Formula for nearly everything.

Once the résumé was finalized I decided to ship it off to a few companies. I figured it would work as another test drive before I went after Empyrean.

I spent more and more time in the library as my résumés made their way through the bureaucratic jungle. I read books on avoiding "job hell." Patrick Lenconi's *The Three Signs of a Miserable Job* was one of my favorites. He spoke at length of "the three key principles that make work miserable: irrelevance, immeasurability, and anonymity." And he was correct with these three. Extremely correct. I remembered one job that I had waiting tables in a restaurant. The manager didn't care about his staff and treated most of us like robots. Lenconi's book was dead on, and I'd make sure to watch for these signs in all my future job interviews.

Part Two

A perfectly warm afternoon came and I was sitting on the front terrace admiring the sunset. I was finished reading for the day and felt exhausted from my weeklong excursion at the library.

The trees were beginning to bud and an early summer seemed to be just around the bend. A young woman jogged past. I recognized her from class. She waved. I waved back. Things were good. I breathed deep to taste the heat, and sighed with great exuberance at how well I was doing with my work.

My cell phone vibrated. For a moment I contemplated ignoring it, but I reached in through the front door and removed it from the table. I checked the number. I had no idea who this was.

"Great…" I said. Probably another telemarketer… "Hello?"

"Hi, Adrian Addler?"

"May I ask who is calling?"

"This is Bryce Halbersen from International Western Consultation. I am calling in regards to your application."

"Yes, sir, this is Adrian Addler. How are you doing?" I could barely contain my excitement. I had been willing to take the risk, and now it was paying off.

"I'm fine, thank you. Do you have a few minutes to go over your qualifications?"

"Sure I do," I said. "What questions could I answer for you?"

"You've been an intern at J&J for how many years?"

"I've been working with them for just under two years. Have you had a chance to look at the list on my résumé detailing the achievements I've made during those two years?"

"Yes, I have. I must say, I'm very impressed. We have one associate position that we're looking to fill right now at IWC. I was wondering if you would be interested in coming in for an interview. The job involves working with our special-projects division. You'd be assisting the project team in organizing and executing seven promotional campaigns throughout the fiscal year. There's definitely plenty of opportunity for growth here at

IWC, not to mention we start all our fresh recruits with competitive salaries."

If this wasn't a classic case of demonstrating Signs of Interest (SOIs), I didn't know what was.

"Yes sir, I'd definitely be interested. When would you like to meet?"

"How about Monday, April 4th? Is there a certain time that would fit your schedule best? I see that you're still in school."

That was three days after Empyrean was going to start accepting applications. It felt funny that everything was happening at once. Then, I remembered what Tammy Turner said in her presentation: Schedule it for the morning.

"How about first thing?" I said.

"I can do 9:15 a.m."

"9:15 it is."

We said our goodbyes and hung up. Bingo. If landing an interview at IWC was that easy, I knew I would have no problem getting one at Empyrean.

*   *   *

I was sitting at about $100 in my bank account and had a $10 bill in my wallet. I was still waiting to hear from Potter & Sons, but I felt good about my prospects with IWC. I only had to wait another week before I could apply to Empyrean, and that week couldn't pass soon enough.

It felt good to be in demand. I must have been doing something right.

It was Friday night and I went down to the Strawberry Street Market and perused the beer selection. I needed to go with something cheap, but I couldn't bring myself to touch the Natty Light. Well, then again, I couldn't be too picky. Besides, I had to replace the beers I drank from Emily's stash.

I reached into the freezer, pulled out a 12-pack, and slid the glass shut. The bells on the market door chimed. I looked up, caught the glimpse of high heels, a knee-length skirt, long brunette hair, perfect eyes—and she was looking at yours truly. I stood up straight, Natty Light in hand, and breathed deep.

I suddenly realized that I was staring at Isabelle.

*   *   *

I snapped my attention to the wall. She approached the beer freezer. Quickly I turned and set my case of Natty on the floor. This way maybe I could pretend to be searching for a more refined brew.

She stood right next to me, both of us searching the dozens of beers for something appetizing. A moment later she turned to walk behind me and stumbled, catching herself on a shelf of soda cans. She had tripped on my case of Natural Ice... wonderful...

"I'm sorry," I said, fumbling to pick up the beer. I looked down, avoided eye contact, and pretended to straighten the rack of soda.

"Do I know you from somewhere?" she asked.

"Um, yeah, maybe... I'm Adrian Addler. I think we met a few weeks ago at Baron's Pub."

"Oh yeah..."

"You're Isabelle, right?" I said. I looked into her eyes for the first time since the bar. The isles of vegetables and potato chips faded into an obscure blob of swirling colors. Her hair, her nails, her skin, her voice... I absorbed all of it like a sponge.

"You never called me," she said.

"I, well... I haven't had the time. What with exams right before break and—"

"Where did you go for break? You couldn't have called me then?"

It was horrible. The most beautiful girl in town and here she was, practically beating the door down to go out with me and I couldn't afford to drop the dime. Damn... I needed a job. "I've been busy all break. You know, looking for a job and whatnot. I've got some interviews lined up for early next week and I've been prepping, spending a lot of time in the library, you know."

"I see..." she wasn't convinced, but she wasn't angry. "I also see that you're doing a lot of studying tonight." She pointed at the 12-pack.

"Um, yeah, this is just for my apartment. I like to keep a couple in the fridge."

"You live with some freshmen frat boys or something? I thought people quit drinking Natty shortly after their second year in college?" she chuckled.

"Well, my friend Jake drinks most of the beer. I'm more of a wine guy myself," I said. I headed over to the wine section, no idea what I was talking about, grabbed a bottle of something called Renaissance Revival Chianti, and pretended to study the label for information. There really wasn't anything written on it, so I just stared at the picture—an overweight, half-nude woman painted in some sort of Baroque style (I had taken a few art history classes in my day…).

"You like Chianti?" she asked.

"Only on certain occasions."

"What else do you like?"

"Merlot," I said, "and other red stuff… you know… the usual… Cabernet and Pinot Grigio."

"Pinot Grigio is a white wine," she smiled at me, pushing my shoulder playfully. I looked down at the floor, one hand in my pocket and one hand gripping the beers.

I asked her what she was doing that night. She said she had a family function to go to, that she had stopped in at the market to buy cheese and a fruit platter. I smiled, tried to make conversation about doing something in the future, but in the end I wound up purchasing the wine, the beers, and a bag of horrible-looking crackers that she recommended I try. I was out a solid $22 dollars on pointless crap.

I carried my treasures back to the apartment and sat on the front porch drinking the beers, snacking on crackers, and watching the hours slip away.

*   *   *

That night, around 7:30, just as I was about to get into the shower, my cell phone rang. It was my parents.

I walked inside, went upstairs, into my bedroom, shut the door, sat down on the bed, and listened. My mother was trying to tell me something, but she wouldn't spit it out. There was all this small talk, all this unimportant rambling. I could tell that something was really eating at her.

"Just tell me what's going on, Mom!" I finally said.

"Adrian… it's hard to say this…"

"Come ON!" I was getting impatient.

She took a deep breath and let out a sigh. "Your father's been laid off. It could be permanent, but no one knows. The company is doing horribly. They let go of 50% of their upper-level executives and 30% of the workforce. Dad was among those who were cut."

"Bastards…" I said. "Why would they do that? Dad's been there for 25 years!"

"I know…" She paused. "There's one more thing, Adrian…"

"What's that?"

"We won't be able to make your student-loan payments…"

*   *   *

I stood in silence for a moment. "You're joking," I said finally. I had no idea it would come to this.

"It's either we help you with your loan payments or we lose the house. And you know how much your father wants to retire in this house."

I took a deep breath and sighed it out.

"Well, don't we have any savings money left to help pay off the loans?"

"I'm sorry, Adrian, we don't. We're going to have to pull together as a family. Your father and I think you should pay off your loans yourself once you get your new job… wherever that is."

I hadn't thought there could be any more pressure, and now there was this.

"By the way, how's your job search going?" she asked.

"It's good," I said, unable to think about anything other than this newly incurred debt. It was astonishing, unforeseen, and it would cost most of my salary for the first few years.

I shook my head and stared solemnly at the ceiling.

*   *   *

After spending some time in my room alone, I called Jake. He was convinced that we needed to go down to the Baron's Pub.

"I don't have the money man. Flat out."

"It's fine. It's on me," he said. He met me at the corner and we went walking down the street. We hooked a quick right and yanked the door to the pub. It was locked, a sign written in permanent marker hanging on the glass: CLOSED FOR SPRING BRAKE. RENOVATION IN PROGRESS.

Jake laughed, "They misspelled 'break.'"

"This place is always nasty anyway…"

"Let's go down to the Fusion Lounge."

"You sure?" I warned. "Fusion's pretty pricey…"

"Don't worry about it, man. Like I said, it's on me."

"Alright. If you say so…"

PART THREE

Fusion was fairly quiet. It was still a bit early, and Jake and I took a seat and ordered up a couple beers. We drank them down. In the soft light of orange and red lamps that glowed warmly on each table we could see several older men in suits laughing in a corner booth. A very attractive middle-aged woman came through the door and took a seat at the bar a few stools down from me.

I breathed in the smell of perfume and vermouth, ran my fingers through my hair, and stared at my blurry reflection in the lacquered surface of the bar.

"Shoot," Jake said, checking his watch just as the second round of beers was arriving. "Sorry man, but I gotta go. I forgot I'm supposed to pick up this girl in 15 minutes."

"Come on, man, we just got here…"

"Sorry, but I gotta do this. Here's $20."

"That's too much," I said.

"It's fine, give me the change tomorrow… I gotta run."

"Thanks, man. Good luck."

I looked down the bar, past the chrome beer tap, past the tired old businessman diving into a scotch and water, past the countless rows of empty glasses. I glanced back to my right, and the woman several stools down caught my eye. I immediately averted my gaze and concentrated on my beer.

"Tough day?" the woman asked.

I looked to my right and saw her for the first time in good light. It was mind-numbing how beautiful she was.

"I'm doing OK," I said.

"You look kind of down."

"Nah, I'm OK."

"What's your name?" she asked.

"Adrian," I said. "You?"

"Jamie."

We shook hands across the empty stools and began a conversation. The guys in the corner were being very loud, so I slid down a couple stools and settled in next to her.

"So, Adrian," she said. "When do you intend on going back there and talking to that girl?"

"What?"

"Don't look now, but the girl in that booth has been eyeing you for the past 15 minutes."

"No she hasn't…"

"Yes, she has."

This woman was pulling my strings. I turned around, locked eyes with a beautiful early-twenties vixen, and turned back to the bar.

"Told you," she said. "Go on over there and say something."

I stared into the reflection of the bar mirror and could see the girls. They were still staring at me. Oh boy…

I looked at this beautiful woman sitting next to me, mid-40s, sophisticated, well dressed, good personality, and I wondered why she was talking to me in the first place.

"What's bothering you?" she asked. "Any other guy would have gone over there by now."

The beers had loosened me up. I explained the whole situation with my dad's job, my school loans, everything. She seemed impressed. "That's pretty heavy stuff," she said. "I'm glad you've got some interviews coming up."

"That's the silver lining," I said.

"Do you do anything for fun? You have a girlfriend?"

"No, I don't have a girlfriend. For fun I've been volunteering at this place called *Charity | Wells*. I go up there several times a week and train new volunteers and make phone calls. It's pretty cool and gives me good leadership experience, but I sometimes feel like I should be spending my extra time honing my job hunting skills."

"I know what you mean," she said. "I think I've got an idea." She gently put her hand on my shoulder and locked eyes with me. "Do you like to people watch?"

"Uhh… sure," I said. "I do it all the time." I didn't want to look stupid in front of her, so I exaggerated a bit.

"Great! This'll be easy for you then. I'm going to teach you my *favorite* bar game." She must have sensed I was still down about my father losing his job. It was nice of her to try to think of ways to cheer me up.

"Sure, what's the game?" I asked, playing along with her antics. It was embarrassing to have a beautiful woman sitting beside me and still be in a poor mood.

"It's simple. Tell me what you think of that couple over there." She pointed at a guy and a girl sitting in the corner.

"I don't know. They look like an average couple to me."

"I think they're on their first date. What's more, I think he's struggling. I can read it from a mile away."

"How do you know that?"

"I just know."

"There's no way you can tell that just by looking at them... No way."

"Yeah way."

"I don't buy it."

"How much you wanna bet?" she laughed, sensing a feeling of competition between us.

"Well, I'm not really the gambling type..."

"Come on..."

"It's not worth it."

"OK," she said, as though she were thinking of something else. "Alright, I got it: No money. If I win, you have to approach that girl at the table behind us who's been staring at you *all* night."

"And what if I win?" I asked.

"I'll buy you a drink."

We laughed. "That doesn't seem very fair to me."

"Come on..."

"You gotta do better than that," I said. "One drink isn't cutting it."

"Alright, how about this: If you win, I'll buy you another drink AND I'll show you something that will help with those interviews you have next week."

"What can you show me?" I asked.

"Let's just say it's not something you can read in any of those books you've been studying all spring break."

"OK," I said somewhat skeptically, but I was willing to try anything at this point. "Deal."

Jamie grabbed a waitress and leaned close to her ear. She briefly explained that she needed the waitress' help in determining the outcome of a bet. The waitress laughed, obviously more intrigued by our antics than by the nightly grind of her serving occupation.

"OK, I'll figure it out," the waitress said.

We watched as she delivered their next round of drinks and struck up a conversation. A few moments later, as she breezed past us, she looked at me and smiled.

"Looks like you lost this one, buddy." She winked and looked at the girls in the booth behind us.

I shook my head and asked Jamie how she knew.

"Let's just say I had a hunch. Now, get over there and talk to that girl."

I stood up, my nerves coursing through my bones like fast electric shocks. I imagined my failure, my rejection, my inability to formulate sentences. It was horrible. I almost turned around halfway, but I figured I had to complete my end of the bet.

I approached the booth like the Tin Man in *The Wizard of Oz* and said the first thing that came to my mind, which was an incredibly corny and pathetic pickup line.

"Excuse me, do I know you from somewhere?"

PART FOUR

The girl looked up from her half-empty Mandarin blossom Cosmo and scrunched her eyebrows. Before she spoke, before even a word came through her lips, she looked me up and down. "I don't think so," she said.

I stood there stone silent, a man on the firing line waiting for a barrage of bullets. My palms were sweating profusely and my heart beat like a tribal drum. After one or two minutes, the dull and uninteresting conversation dried up.

"Well, I gotta get back to my friend at the bar," I said. "Nice talking to you two."

"Yeah," they said.

I walked back to the bar, to my lukewarm beer, and took the last hard chug.

"How did it go?"

"Honestly? Not very well."

"I could sense that much," she said. "Let me let you in on a little secret."

"What's that?"

"It's about your body language."

"What about it?"

"This is something that will apply in the bar as well as in your job-hunting expeditions."

"But I didn't win the bet. You only had to tell me if you lost."

"That's fine. You're a good sport. I like you."

"Sounds good to me," I said. The bartender arrived and took my empty pint glass. He slid another one toward me. I smiled, grabbing a fresh, frothy, beautiful lager and taking the first pull.

"I have to say, I applaud you for attempting something like that, but your problem was all in your approach. I don't want to sound harsh, but you blew it from the very beginning. You looked like Eeyore, the donkey from Winnie the Pooh, on your way over to the table."

I was embarrassed, but I was still able to laugh at myself. "I honestly don't know what got into me. I just kind of froze up."

Jamie took another sip of her beer. "That's because you were under an extreme amount of stress. Now, I'm going to get a little deep here, but try to follow along because what I'm going to tell you will dramatically decrease the level of anxiety you have before interacting with people. I call it my *Anxiety Annihilator*."

"Alright," I said, leaning in a little closer, as the bar had started to fill up a little more.

"So, the human body responds to stress in three ways: physically, emotionally, and mentally. Your physical stress was displayed in the tension in your body and in the girls' bodies. Tension is contagious. When you tense it drains your energy *and* the group's energy. Remember that.

"Your emotional stress was apparent in the level of anxiety you showed when I saw you approach them. The fear of rejection and any other negative feelings you might've experienced was enough to prevent most guys from even attempting the task. But I'm glad you second-guessed yourself and went through with it anyway.

"Finally, your mental stress, or worry, probably acted like roadblocks and prevented you from saying anything charming or witty while you were actually in front of those girls. Remember this: When emotion goes up, intelligence goes down."

I was impressed. Jamie had described *exactly* what was going on in my body. I knew that overcoming stress was something I needed to work on. After all, this entire job-searching process was extremely taxing, and every interview was taking a lot out of me. I contemplated for a few more seconds before asking, "So, what do I have to do to overcome this kind of tension?"

Jaime cracked a smile. "Have you ever tried relaxing?"

I was befuddled by her question. "Of course... I've relaxed all the time. Who hasn't?"

"Yes, but can you tell me how you do it?"

Why does it always seem that the questions that seem so simple are always the hardest to answer?

"Umm... I just lay down, I guess. Watch TV or something."

"That's not relaxing, that's just hanging out. Relaxation needs to be intentional. You need to remember that tension is unconscious, so we have to consciously relax to get rid of it. To fully relax, you must start with both feet firmly on the floor. This grounds you and reminds you that you are in the moment.

"Okay..." I said. My foot couldn't plant firmly on the floor when I was sitting in the barstool, so I had to stand up.

"Alright, now you can close your eyes if you want. It will help you concentrate.

I felt a bit funny standing in a bar with my eyes closed in front of a beautiful woman, but I had already made a huge ass of myself. Why stop there?

"Now, I'm sure you know the rules about proper breathing. Inhale through your nose, exhale through your mouth, right?"

"Yes," I said.

"So, inhale for three seconds and exhale for six. Part of the reason we feel stress is because we never allow our lungs to fully exhale. We walk around with our lungs half-full most of the time. That is why you exhale longer than you inhale."

I had already done this several times, counting the seconds in my head, before I felt the effects of this exercise. I immediately felt more comfortable in my setting.

I sat back down on the stool and almost felt like a new person. "Wow, I'm totally doing this before my next job interview. I feel so relaxed."

Jaime laughed. "Everyone says something like that. It's funny how it has the same effect on every person."

"So, what are you? Some sort of body-language expert or something?"

"Well, not exactly... Let's just say that body language plays an important role in my occupation."

"What do you do for a living?"

"Guess."

Hmm... this would be hard. She was beautiful, confident, intelligent; there was any number of things she could have been. "Um... maybe a salesperson?"

"Good try, but no. Although, sales is one of my strong points."

"Alright... not a salesperson... hmm..." I took another sip of the beer. "You used to be a fashion model."

She jolted with laughter. "Flattering, Adrian, but no."

"OK, I give up. What do you do?"

"I'm a professional Wing-Woman."

Wing-Woman? Was she in the Air Force? I had no idea what this could mean. She sensed my lack of understanding.

"What do you think a Wing-Woman does?" she asked.

"I don't know... Are you like an escort or something?"

She laughed again. "No, but I get that a lot. I'm a dating coach for men—like a female version of Hitch. I meet with men in a bar setting and teach them how to act around women. I tell them what women want and how they perceive a man's actions. It's like having an insider's perspective of what goes on inside a female's mind when you're trying to pick her up."

"I see..."

"The skills I focus on with 99% of my clients have to do with body language. And, as is evident from watching your attempt earlier, you have some issues you need to work on. Relaxation is a start, but that alone isn't going to cut it."

"OK, where do I start?"

"Well, you said you have some interviews coming up, right? Well, in the interviewing world there is a universal code of body language. It doesn't matter if you're a man or woman, you have to put forth essentially the same movements in order to come across as a desirable candidate."

I nodded my head. I had been a bit skeptical, but there was definitely a part of me that wanted to know more.

"The trick to any successful interaction is knowing how to display confident body language. In addition to this, you must be able to read body language accurately. Now, I'm not going to be able to go into detail on everything you'll need to know, but I'll give you enough so that you'll be able to go into your next interview with some skills that will help you win over your interviewer."

"Sounds good to me," I said with enthusiasm. Things were starting to look up.

"The first thing you need to know is that body language is an outward reflection of a person's emotional condition. Women, being far more emotionally developed than men, are literally 10 times more perceptive of body language. This means that you have to look good in front of men, but you have to look *especially* good in front of women."

"Right..." I said, remembering my awkward interaction with Isabelle just a few hours prior. I knew that she must have seen me as such a wuss.

"The next thing you need to know is that people have emotional reactions to those individuals who have higher value than them, or in other cases, those who have a threat to their value. For example, think about the last time you met an attractive woman, or the last time you were in the presence an authority figure like a cop or the hiring manager at your last job interview."

I continued to think about what had happened a few hours ago with Isabelle. She took a sip of her beer. I did the same. The bar began to fill even more and we had to speak a bit louder to hear one another.

"When you're in a job interview, or in any social interaction, there is always one person who is reacting more than the others. Those who do not react are usually more confident and composed. Confidence and composure are signs of higher status, and the majority of people are pre-wired to be attracted to high status.

I nodded. She could tell that I didn't totally get it.

"Just think Brad Pitt in *Troy* versus Brad Pitt in *Burn After Reading*. Which role would you say communicated higher status?"

"*Troy*..." I said. The gears were turning in my head. "OK, I see... so, composure is the way to communicate higher status?"

"Right. You have to remain composed..."

She could tell that I was trying to wrap my head around this. "Here's another example: The other day I walk onto the elevator of an accounting firm to meet a client and there was a guy already inside, standing next to elevator buttons. He was dressed like he was going to the office from the gym. He was still in his gym clothes, but it was a Saturday, so I figured that was pretty normal. Despite his clothing, he had well-groomed hair, a shaved face, clean fingernails... you know, he looked successful."

I formulated a picture of this guy in my head and she continued. "Then another guy comes bumbling into the elevator. He was overweight, dressed in a cheap suit, his briefcase bursting with papers, his shirt wasn't tucked in. His face was shiny like a cue ball and the top of his head was a sweaty mess."

I laughed, envisioning the guy in gym clothes staring at him, wondering, "What the hell is this guy's problem?"

"So, this sweaty man's body language and demeanor just screamed that he wasn't 'with it,' so to speak." She took another sip from the beer. "Next, our bumbling accountant friend, briefcase nearly bursting at the seams, looks over to the guy standing next to the elevator buttons and says 'fifth floor.'

"Our gym guy, still perplexed by this man's erratic behavior, presses the fifth-floor button. Then, the accountant realizes he said 'fifth floor,' not 'fifth floor, please.' I can tell that he feels bad. 'Sorry, I didn't mean to come across like a jerk,' he says, still kind of fidgeting around.

"The other guy sort of just looks at him, says, 'No problem,' and turns away, totally ignoring his existence for the rest of the ride."

"I'd have done the same thing," I said.

"Right, unless YOU were the bumbling accountant and didn't realize it."

I sat there and remembered my interaction with Isabelle in the Strawberry Street Market. I had made a fool of myself without even realizing it. She must have thought I was nervous as hell... I had avoided eye contact, kept my hand in my pocket, and stared at the floor the entire time.

Jamie continued, "Within 15 seconds, I knew everything I needed to know. The guy in gym clothes, I'd trust him to be my attorney or accountant. The bumbling idiot... well, let's just say I wouldn't trust him to look after my dog," she laughed. "It's all about body language and composure."

I could tell that Jamie had experience teaching this stuff. She flowed so smoothly through the story and it seemed so real and thought-out, yet not at all rehearsed.

"I'm sorry for rambling, Adrian," she said, eyeing the empty beer glasses. "This is what happens when I get on a roll. I get into coaching mode."

I looked down at the glasses, fingered the $20 bill from Jake, and waved at the bartender. Jake would understand...

"You got any dates you need to keep?" I asked Jamie.

"Not until 10."

"You want another beer?"

"I'd love one."

I waved at the bartender and within a moment we were ready to roll.

"What else can you tell me about body language?" I asked. I was transfixed by this unexpected conversation with an intelligent, beautiful, composed woman. I wished that the night would never end, that the beers would flow until morning, and that I would walk away a smarter and more knowledgeable man.

PART FIVE

Jamie surveyed the filling bar. A man smiled at her and she waved. "Former client," she said. "He's with a pretty girl. Talk about a satisfied customer..."

"Alright, where to continue? You're applying for a job, you need to impress people..." She was thinking, rolling her eyes to the ceiling and trying to formulate another lesson. "Ah-ha, let's talk about first impressions: People will immediately begin to evaluate your credibility within the first seven seconds after you walk in the door. They do this based on your clothes. Ninety percent of their opinion of you will be made in the first five or so minutes, and 60 to 80% of the impact you will make is non-verbal.

"Women will look at a male candidate's hair length, clothes design, color coordination, the creases in his trousers, shine on his shoes, and last but not least... the dimple in his tie."

"I had no idea people really looked at all that stuff."

"It's scary, Adrian, but they do. And what's worse: It gets even more detailed for women. A woman will notice *everything* about another woman. Men are easier. A male interviewer will only check the shine of another man's shoes and the dimple in his tie. However, male interviewers will check out the chest, legs, and butt of a woman."

"I'm not surprised," I agreed.

"Neither am I... Even in a supposedly 'equal' business world, this is the reality that we live in. You can't blame men, though. They can't help that that's how their brains are wired."

"So, other than dress, how do I exhibit confidence?"

"Lift your chest, put your shoulders back, and tilt your head back." She touched my shoulders and stood me up once again. The girls at the table behind us were staring. Honestly, I didn't care.

"You want to take up space and be comfortable with your power. Project yourself, and above all, maintain good eye contact."

"This feels awkward," I said.

"Well, it doesn't have to be quite so... dramatic. But, then again, whenever you learn a new habit it's going to feel awkward. The thing is this:

You're used to doing it the wrong way. You need to exaggerate a little bit to make it feel... natural."

I stood there like a dummy, pushing my chest out, my shoulders back, tilting my head, moving my arms around. I think the bartender was watching me and snickering. Perhaps this was a weekly occurrence?

"It'll take you some time to get rid of your nervous ticks. You know, things like eyes that dart around, leaning in when speaking, weak hand shakes, looking down. These behaviors will telegraph too much interest and translate into lower value."

"Wow, I never really knew that it was such a problem."

"Most people don't."

She took another sip, and in mid-swallow remembered something she had left out. As she gulped she extended an open palm to signal to me that she wasn't finished yet.

"The interview, as with any first time meeting, is about building rapport with the other person.

"A way to do this without the other person being consciously aware of what you are doing is to use a method known as the *Mirroring-Matching* technique. It's called Mirror-Matching because you want to *mirror* the other person's body language and *match* their voice tonalities and speed of speaking. If his or her shoulders or forearms are resting on the table, make sure yours are, as well. The idea is that the more you are able to imitate the behaviors and mannerisms of your interviewer, the more comfortable he or she will become with you and the more you will be seen as a peer, rather than a candidate."

"So, I basically want to turn myself into a carbon copy of the other person?"

"Don't take it too far, but yes. Think about things like speaking at the same pace, the same volume, and with the same tone. This will help match your personality to theirs. Researchers have done studies that show very interesting things about this. For example, if I was to sit here and talk extremely fast about research conducted at the university," the speed of her voice increased, "and was to tell you that speaking quickly would," she got even faster, "make your interviewer overwhelmed and possibly even agitated, you would probably begin to wonder why I was throwing so much information at you after only knowing you for such a short period of time."

We laughed. "I see what you mean. It is a tendency for me to start speaking faster whenever I'm nervous."

"It's a problem for most people," she said.

"Speaking of most people," I pointed across the bar, "how did you know that that couple was on their first date?"

"Well, I could tell you, Adrian, but then I'd have to kill you..." she said this very seriously.

I knew she was yanking my chain, so I followed along just for fun.

"OK... never mind then." I said.

"I'm kidding. Let me see, how do I explain this?" She looked at the door, as if she was expecting someone. I didn't bother to ask. It was getting close to 10 o'clock. "It's pretty easy to tell when you've people watched as much as I have. People have things called Tells that reveal secrets about their psychology."

I was curious if Jamie's definition of Tells were the same as Tammy's definition of Signs of Interest. I kept listening to see if I could make a match.

"The first Tell I noticed was that the guy was sitting squarely facing the woman. He was leaning in, wide-eyed, and talking about something that wasn't really interesting the girl."

I looked over at the couple and observed what she was describing. "I think I've done that before..." I said.

"Most guys do. Tell number two: The girl was sitting at a 45-degree angle, legs crossed away from the guy." I looked over again and witnessed this display in action. Jamie was right on.

"And finally, Tell number three: She was smiling with her mouth, not with her eyes."

"Smiling with your eyes?"

"Yes. A natural smile produces wrinkles around the eyes. Insincere people smile only with their mouth."

She demonstrated this and I could blatantly see the difference. I was impressed.

"So anyway, the girl was sitting at a 45-degree angle, which is sort of a neutral zone, not really interested and not really disinterested. This leads me to believe that she wasn't totally comfortable around her date. You see, when you sit at a 45-degree angle, you also subconsciously increase your perceived value to whomever you're speaking with because they haven't won your approval yet. You should definitely do this in your interview."

"That's cool. I had no idea, but I guess I see what you mean. This stuff really does make sense."

"I know, that's why I do this for a living. I LOVE it. Keep in mind that people don't value what they don't work for. In other words, don't telegraph too much interest until they've earned it. But, then again, don't be so cocky about yourself that you repel an employer from wanting you on their team. No one likes a big swingin' dick..."

The bartender had heard this last remark and the three of us laughed.

"One last thing: It helps to remember that one body language mistake won't make or break your interview or interaction with a girl. It's the summation of these behaviors that tells the unconscious brain whether or not it should be attracted to you. So, if you mess up once, just brush it off and refocus your attention on creating attraction."

"Got it." I thought back to what had happened with Isabelle. Did this mean that I had a chance at correcting my mistakes next time I saw her?

Jamie looked at the doorway and I turned around. A nerdy-looking business man, a direct knockoff version of Bill Gates, walked mechanically into the bar. He removed his glasses and squinted at the room.

"That's my 10 o'clock," Jamie said.

"It was nice talking to you. Thanks for all the help."

"No problem." She handed me a business card and told me to give her a call if I ever needed anything.

"Will do," I said.

"You're a bright kid, Adrian. And I can tell that you're a good person. I have a feeling you'll be pleasantly surprised with what the universe has in store for you."

She walked toward the door and I turned back to the bar. It was about time I went home as well. It had been a long day and I needed a few cups of water and a good sleep. I finished the beer and stared at Jamie's half-full pint glass.

Did I say half full?

Yeah... half full.

THE WORST THING YOU CAN
POSSIBLY DO IN A DEAL IS
SEEM DESPERATE TO MAKE IT.
THAT MAKES THE OTHER GUY
SMELL BLOOD, AND THEN
YOU'RE DEAD.

....

–DONALD J. TRUMP
Chairman and CEO of the Trump Organization

CHAPTER 6

THE INNER CIRCLE

The gears of the world were turning and I found myself on the brink of making the biggest decision of my life. Every little choice I made had to be analyzed carefully because I was supporting myself. Ever since I had received the news of my father's layoff, I had felt an overbearing sense of responsibility, something that pushed me even harder to succeed on my own.

The first of April could not have come at a more appropriate time. I had subconsciously assumed that this fateful day would never arrive, but here I was: in my cultural anthropology class with my laptop open, one click away from sending my résumé to Empyrean, and one day away from interviewing with IWC. I looked up at the clock in the classroom. I had 10 minutes.

Typically, I liked this class, but today's lecture was beyond boring. Professor Stafford, despite being one of the most interesting and well-traveled members of the university faculty, had presented a very dry article and instructed us to read it during class. Needless to say, I had more important things to do…

"Alright," Ms. Stafford said. I looked up from my laptop. "I finally finished grading your term papers and they are ready to be handed back. Sorry it took me so long."

I quickly pulled up the assigned article in case Stafford decided to take a glance at my laptop on the way past.

"How do you think you did?" I heard one guy ask another.

"Alright," the other guy said. "I didn't really understand the assignment."

The assignment had been to explain and dissect one piece of oral history from any cultural group in the world. Emily had told me how important this paper was, and she had given me her paper as a sample to use in deciding my topic. I had thus chosen to write about an Inuit story, a tale which has been termed in modern-day America as "The Tale of the Alaskan Black Wolf."

Stafford handed me the paper with a smile. I flipped it over and saw 97% written in red. I was thrilled. I had busted my ass on this paper and knew that it deserved a good grade. I sighed and slid the paper into my bag. This was certainly a load off my back. I couldn't think of a better day: I got a good grade on this paper *and* I was applying to Empyrean.

I reopened the page on my laptop and checked the job posting one more time to verify the correct email address. I noticed something I had never seen before: a request for a writing sample. There were no specifications about what the sample should entail, but it was made known that school essays were acceptable. I looked down at my anthropology paper and decided that a 97% was not too bad, so, when I submitted my résumé and cover letter, I also attached the electronic copy I had saved on my computer.

"Alright, folks," Professor Stafford announced. "That will be all for today. Please finish reading..." I put my finger on the ENTER key. I took a deep, purposeful breath, a breath I had been waiting to take for several months, and pulled the trigger.

Two beautiful words flashed on the screen: "Message Sent."

Immediately after submitting my résumé, cover letter, and writing sample, I realized I had made the right choice. It was almost as if the light bulb went off in my head, a total "a-ha!" moment. I knew exactly how I was going to approach the Empyrean interview, but I would need to get some practice under my belt with IWC. I just hoped it wouldn't blow up in my face.

I walked downstairs and cruised into the atrium. I passed the librarians and the other students. Several of my classmates were discussing something with our professor. I was usually interested in scoring extra points with my professor, but today I didn't stop to shoot the breeze.

My phone rang. It was Emily.

"Hey Emily, I just got out of class."

"We still going to the gym?"

"Yeah, I'll be home in a few minutes."

I drove home and waited in the driveway. She came outside and got into the car.

"Jake called me," I told her. "He said he wants to lift today. I'm going to pick him up real quick."

"That sounds good," she said. "How are things going for you on the job hunt?"

"Alright," I said. "I sent an application to Empyrean today during class. That was pretty sweet."

"Hell yeah!"

"And I got a 97% on my anthropology paper, the one you helped me with."

"I knew that the Alaskan Black Wolf story was a good idea. How are you feeling about the IWC interview? You nervous?"

"Not so much. I'm pretty excited to use some of the techniques I learned from Jamie, that woman from the bar. I'm trying to develop a more professional persona. I think I'm doing a pretty good job."

"That's good," Emily said. "I'm just surprised that you needed some cougar to hit on you in order to realize the importance of body language."

I chuckled, "She wasn't a 'cougar.' She was a professional wingwoman. And she wasn't hitting on me. She does stuff like that for a living."

"Uh-huh…" Emily joked.

I slowed to a stop, flicked on my hazards, and waited for Jake. He came jogging through the front door and down the steps.

"Hey, man," he said. "You send your résumé to Empyrean?"

"Yeah. About 15 minutes ago."

"Sweet," Jake said. "Good luck with that."

I merged back into traffic and drove several miles to the gym. We walked inside and Emily headed toward the cardio room. Jake and I went for the weights.

"Look at that," he said, pointing out of the weight room at one of the elliptical machines. There was a girl doing a cardio workout, her shirt rolled up high and her stomach exposed.

"Dude…those have to be fake…" I said.

"Whatever man… if you can touch 'em, they're real…" I chuckled at Jake's obsession and took a seat on the bench.

I found myself unable to focus on the weights. I couldn't stop thinking about IWC and, more importantly, Empyrean. How would I act in the interviews? What would I say? What stories would I tell?

I took a deep breath and tried to focus. I had to stop obsessing over these jobs. I couldn't be daydreaming about my career future while I was in the weight room. I'd never get anything accomplished this way.

We loaded some weights on the incline bench and Jake took the first set. It was a futile effort to keep my mind off of the job hunt. I kept thinking about my past interviews, about all the things I'd done both right and wrong. Emily had been right when she told me that interviewing was a skill. It took time, practice, and dedication to get to where I was. Now, after all this practice, I had finally made a move on my dream job.

*   *   *

I unlocked the door, jimmied the handle, and walked inside.

"That door handle is broken again," I yelled to Emily, who was in the kitchen. "Be careful not to get your key stuck. I'll call the maintenance guy tomorrow."

"OK," she said, and when I was halfway up the stairs she continued, "There's a letter for you on the table."

I stopped mid-stride. There were only a handful of people who would be sending me a letter: the credit card company, my parents, or the two companies I had interviewed with several weeks back. If it was my parents, or if it looked like junk mail, Emily wouldn't have said anything. Anticipation built as I set my gym bag on the steps and walked briskly into the kitchen.

"Where is it?" I asked, slightly impatient. I immediately saw the letter and picked it up. I scanned the return address: Potter & Sons Inc…

"Who is it from?" she asked.

"A company I interviewed with last week. Damn, that was fast."

I opened the envelope. My jaw dropped. My hard work had paid off. "They offered me a decent salary, plus a $200 a month stipend."

"And that's Potter & Sons?"

"Yeah. They're not the best company I applied to—remember the half-empty case of beer I told you about?—but at least I'm getting some positive results."

"That's great," Emily said, putting her arm on my shoulder and reading the letter with me. "You should really try to negotiate the salary. Not to mention the stipend. Health insurance doesn't seem that important right now, but it will be extremely important in the long run. One time I broke my finger and got a $2,500 bill because I was between insurance policies."

"Damn…"

"How do I negotiate the salary?"

"You should see if you can get a hold of Robert. He would be willing to give you some pointers. I could explain it, but I think he gets a kick out of helping young people. Honestly, I don't think that he sees himself as being much older than either of us."

I went up to my room, checked my email, looked at a few books, and sat down on my bed to call Robert.

"Hey, Robert, it's Adrian Addler."

"Hey, man," he said. He seemed excited to hear from me. "What's going on?"

"Not much. I was wondering if you had a few minutes?"

"Yeah, what do you need?"

I asked him if he minded giving me some advice on salary negotiations and he said that he would be glad to. Instead of doing it over the phone, however, he wanted me to meet him that Saturday afternoon at the Dominion Club to play tennis.

"Tennis?" I said, unsure what to do. I was a horrible tennis player. Honestly, I'd played about five games in my life, three of which were in high school gym class, and all of them had been a disaster. I was sufficiently strong, but I wasn't the most agile person when it came to running around a green square for two hours.

"Yeah, I'd love to play." Funny how words just... come out.

"Good! An old friend of mine is coming as well. It'll be a blast. Then, afterwards, we can talk shop."

"OK. See you then," I said.

My God... what had I done? I'd make a fool of myself. Then again, who really gave a damn? I could hang with some old dudes on the tennis court, and so what if I made a couple of mistakes? I was in decent shape, had a strong arm... what could go wrong?

PART TWO

I pulled up at the tennis court, popped my trunk, and removed a racquet and tube of balls. Lucky for me, Emily's boyfriend, Josh, had let me borrow his tennis equipment.

"Hey Adrian," Robert shouted from the court. He and another man were wrapping up what looked like a warm-up set. There was a woman stretching in the grass a few yards away.

She looked up at me, smiled, and waved.

Robert walked through the gate, followed by a man in his mid-50's. "Adrian, this is Bill Blanchard. He's an old friend of mine."

"Nice to meet you," I said, shaking his hand firmly. The man was fairly tall, well built, and looked like a younger version of Joe Biden. He looked into my eyes very sharply as we shook, and I could sense an overwhelming surge of knowledge and strength.

"I haven't seen Bill in probably, what, three years?" he looked at Bill in question.

"It's been three years and two months," Bill said. "Because the last time we saw each other was on my anniversary weekend." His deep and resonating voice, his strong presence, and his surety all led me to believe that he was a very savvy and intelligent person.

Robert pointed toward the woman in the grass, smiled, and said, "Adrian, I'd like you to meet my girlfriend, Elaine Palmer."

"Hi, Elaine, nice to meet you," I said. She stood and approached me, brushing some loose grass off of her skirt.

"Nice to meet you too, Adrian," she said, extending her hand. I shook it, meeting her eyes and realizing why Robert had needed a babysitter all those nights…

We played a warm-up set and very quickly commenced our first game. I was startled at how well I was doing. I was really getting into the game. Heck, I was doing alright… I was smacking, spinning, running across the court like a young Pete Sampras. At least, this is how it felt to me…

Suddenly, Elaine fell to the ground, clutching her ankle. The three of us jogged over to see what was wrong.

"It's OK," she said, grimacing. "I've done this before..."

"Can I get you some ice?" I asked.

She agreed that she needed some ice. She also thought that she should get out of the heat. I helped her stand up, draped her arm over my shoulder, and together we hobbled across the court.

"You two keep playing," Elaine said. "You haven't seen each other in three years."

Robert and Bill protested.

"Seriously, you guys, Adrian and I can handle this."

We left the court, hobbled up the lawn, and entered the clubhouse dining room. The air conditioning hit me like a ton of bricks. I set Elaine in a chair by the door and ran to the bar. The place was virtually empty. It was two hours before lunchtime, and the bartender was nowhere to be seen. I stepped behind the bar, found a plastic bag full of oranges, dumped the oranges on the counter, filled the bag with ice, and carried it to Elaine.

"Thanks so much," she said. The bag was pressed tightly against her throbbing ankle, and immediately I could see her cringe at the burning sensation caused by the cold. The bartender came back and I told him what I had done.

"No problem," he said. "We're closed right now, so feel free to hang out over there until she feels better. And let me know if you need more ice."

I returned to Elaine with a glass of water. She took several long gulps and set it on the table.

"So, tell me a bit about yourself. I've got to hear something to get my mind off of this ankle."

"Well, I'm about to graduate from college and I am looking for a job."

"Job hunting..." she said. "Always exciting."

"Well, in this economy it's more frustrating than exciting."

"I bet..." she said. "How do you know Robert?"

I explained how I had met him through *Charity | Wells* and how he had mentored me on marketing myself properly to help me land more interviews.

"That sounds like something everyone could use at your age."

"Yeah, it is," I said. "I'm thankful for all the time he's given me." I paused, stared through the window as a distant golfer hit a long ball over the lake. You had to be an exceptional golfer to play on a course like this—otherwise you'd make a fool of yourself.

"How did you meet Robert?" I asked.

"Actually it was several years ago at one of Bill's charity events. Bill does all sorts of charities for people in third-world countries. Talk about generosity... I don't know if Robert told you this, but Bill is an ex-venture capitalist from New York. He spent the first half of his life getting rich, and has spent the last five or so years giving back to the world."

"Sounds cool."

"It is. He's a great guy."

We sat in silence for a few minutes. I asked her if she wanted a towel to put beneath the ice, but she said it was fine the way it was.

"So... what has Robert taught you about how to get a job? I know how much he loves explaining how things work in the business world. God knows I've heard enough from him to write an entire year of articles for *Forbes* magazine."

I chuckled and went over some of the things Robert and I had talked about: how to think like the employer, how to make myself more valuable, etc.

"Just when you think you know it all, a guy like Robert comes along," she laughed.

"Yeah, tell me about it."

"So, Robert said you're in the salary-negotiation process for Potter & whoever?"

"Yeah, Potter & Sons. I'm trying to talk them up a bit."

"You know, that's an area I've got some experience in."

"Really?" My whole outlook on the conversation immediately changed. I found myself sitting up a bit straighter and rolling my shoulders back. I felt like there was a reason Elaine and I were talking.

She briefly explained her experience as a financial analyst for an investment-banking firm. She had put in an unholy amount of hours at work, navigated up the pay scale by job hopping and negotiating salaries, and found herself becoming an early success.

"Most women aren't assertive with negotiating," she said. "That was the difference between me and the other women I competed against. Did you know that 57% of men negotiate for a higher salary and only 7% of women even attempt to bargain for more than what was offered?"

"I had no idea," I said.

"Most women don't realize that a lower starting salary means slower growth during your entire tenure with the company, not to mention the lost opportunity cost of the compounded interest that could've been earned had they gotten a higher starting salary in their first entry-level job."

"Whoa," I said. "I didn't catch all that."

"That's probably because they don't teach you this kind of stuff in school." She shook her head, obviously frustrated with the educational system. "Basically, Adrian, the more money you get at Job One, the more money you will earn in Job Two. This is because most people won't voluntarily leave a job unless their new job pays more. Therefore, if you set your sights higher at Job One, you will consequently receive a higher salary as you move forward with your career and accumulate more money overall."

"That makes sense," I said, carrying her empty glass of water back to the bar. I asked the bartender to refill it and brought it back to the table.

"The first thing you have to learn about salary negotiations is that most employers expect you to negotiate."

"Well, maybe so, but I have such little work experience that I just feel ridiculous asking for more money."

"I understand that, and you don't want to come off looking greedy. You need to do your research. Knowing your Fair Market Value, or FMV, for your specific industry and location will be your strongest weapon of influence during the negotiation. Even if the employer doesn't budge, showing that you've done your research will reinforce their buying confidence. It's a win-win no-brainer for you. Employers like employees who do their research."

I agreed with that, and remembered how unprepared I had been for my first interview at Proteus & Paulson. Times had certainly changed since then...

"So, how do I find out my FMV?"

"Have you ever heard of Salary.com? That website is a good start," she said. She leaned toward the table and peered around the empty dining room, "But I've got a little secret of my own..."

"What's that?" I asked.

PART THREE

She smiled deviously. "I've always asked a recruiter to do a market check on my salary expectations. You have to find a recruiter specifically geared to placing people in your industry, but that shouldn't be too difficult. Once you get somebody who will work with you, have them check your field and let you know what to look for.

"This one is kind of a personal secret of mine, and very few others will have the knowledge or the guts to do it, but it will certainly gain you a competitive edge in the negotiation process."

"I need as much of an edge as I can get."

"In this economy, you basically need to implement every little advantage you hear of in order to succeed. There are ex-brokers waiting tables at Waffle House, ex-lawyers standing in the soup lines... It's a nightmare out there, and you have to be prepared to contend with the level of skill that is abundantly misplaced in today's job market."

"I know what you mean," I told her. "My father recently lost his job."

"I'm sorry to hear that, but honestly I'm not surprised. Companies are getting rid of older employees, either retiring them or giving them the boot for the sake of hiring younger, more technically savvy individuals. Knowing how to interview and negotiate is something that the older generations need to pick up just as much, if not more, than the younger ones."

"Yeah," I said, soaking it all in. Elaine was such an intelligent woman. When I first met Robert I had wondered who a guy like him would go for. I imagined him dating a really hot woman, which Elaine was, but it never crossed my mind how high he would aim intellectually. I guess he really had it together...

"The second thing you need to know is that negotiation is all about supply and demand. If your specialized knowledge is in short supply, demand is stronger. With stronger demand, you have more negotiating power."

"My job situation is the opposite," I said. "There are probably hundreds of applicants from my school who have applied for my number-one job choice at Empyrean." I shook my head and realized the seriousness of my situation.

"There may be hundreds of applicants, but you need to remember not all applicants are of equal value to the employer. The demand for A-Players is always high, but the supply is ALWAYS low. The market is typically saturated with B & C Players."

"What if there are other A-Players applying?" I asked.

"That can hamper your negotiation power. But honestly, there are very few A-Players out there, and you should be able to easily separate yourself from the pack. By the time you're at the negotiation table, if you've successfully demonstrated that you're the only A-player available, your negotiation power to up your salary will be high. On the other hand, if you've demonstrated that you're a B or C-player, or if there are still other A-Players in the mix, your negotiation power will be significantly lower."

"So, I've got to become the best A-Player anyone's ever seen."

"Basically." She took a sip of her water. "Think of yourself as an iPhone," she pulled hers out and set it on the table. "When these things came out they were the cream of the crop. Apple was charging $600 bucks for them—with a plan! Now that it's been a while and the secrets have been leaked, other companies are bringing more competition to the table. Heck, you can get this phone for $100 today."

"So, I need to sell myself as the cream of the crop like Apple did with the iPhone when it first came out."

"Right. That's how you get away with charging ridiculous premiums. Make people realize how important and integral you are to their success. Just remember: People don't long for things that aren't in short supply."

"That's kind of like the supply and demand theory."

"What do you know about supply and demand?" she asked.

"They taught us about it in school. You know, the usual stuff..." I was about to spit some bull, but she continued.

"I'll bet your professors never taught you how supply and demand applied to getting a job, did they?" She shook her head. "Students would be so much more successful if professors focused on how to get by in the real world rather than how to get by in the classroom."

"No argument there," I said.

She repositioned the bag of ice. I looked down and noticed that her ankle was a bit swollen.

"Forget it," she said, referring to the swelling. "Let's focus. I never get to talk about this stuff anymore and it's literally one of my favorite subjects." She sat back in the chair, relaxed, and seemed to be enjoying the process.

I suddenly thought about my offer letter from P&S and realized I had no idea what my FMV even was. I needed to find that out...

"What do I do if they offer me a salary below FMV?" I asked.

"That's a good question. You'll need to figure out your MRI numbers."

"MRI?" I looked at her ankle. "You really think it's that bad?"

"No, Adrian," she laughed at my joke, "Not that kind of MRI. When the interviewer hits you with a set of numbers for your salary you'll want to have a frame of reference for judging those numbers quickly. You'll need to be able to check their offer in your head and ask yourself, 'What will I have at the end of the day after taxes, expenses, retirement, etc.' If you can't do this, you won't be able to tell if their offer is good or bad."

"That makes sense... So what does the MRI stand for?"

"Your 'M' number stands for your Minimum Number. This is the lowest salary you will accept. This means you need to do some budgetary analysis and see what your basic needs are. How much money you need to pay off loans, gas, bills, etc."

A flock of terrible thoughts about debt swarmed throughout my mind. I shook my head to ward them off and continued listening.

"Your 'R' number stands for your Realistic number, or the amount you can accept, that makes you feel you are being adequately compensated for your value. You can also think of the 'R' number as the average salary people make in your position at other companies in your specific industry."

"OK, I get it. I think I know, very roughly, what both of those last numbers are."

"Lastly, your 'I' number stands for your Ideal salary. This should be what the top dogs in your field are making. The higher your value to the employer, the more likely you will be able to achieve your Ideal number. Remember, it is not about what you want, need, or think you deserve—it is all about the value you bring to the company."

"Very well explained," I said. One thing I'd noticed after talking to all of these successful professionals was that nearly every one of them focused on Demonstrating Value.

I noticed that her ice bag had nearly melted and offered to give her another one. She said she would like that. It was an excuse for her to continue the conversation. I went to the bar and had the gentleman give me another bag of ice.

Before I arrived back at the table I came up with another question to ask.

"What should I do if they ask me about my salary requirements? I never know what to say."

"That's a good one. Remember to delay 'money-talk' until the employer's mindset has shifted from Shopper to Buyer."

"I'm not sure I follow?" I said, kneeling and looking at her ankle, which was propped on a chair in front of her.

"Think about your own behavior when you shop. Let's say you were looking for a new pair of shoes."

"OK," I said. I placed the ice over her ankle and returned to my seat. She nodded her thanks, but continued speaking uninterrupted. "You try on a dozen pairs of shoes, searching for just the right look, fit, and feel. In addition to these things, you need to find the qualities that match your needs. So, after an hour of looking, you find the right shoes. They fit well, look great, and have all the features you require.

"It is at this point that you make the transition from Shopper to Buyer. You look down at your feet and imagine these shoes in your daily life. You become emotionally attached to them. You begin to feel that they're yours already."

Elaine continued, "I remember buying a $180 pair of dress shoes when I got my first internship. I had gone into the store with a $140 budget, but after I slipped my feet into those shoes, I knew I would never find anything better. You see, I had switched from a Shopper mentality to a Buyer mentality. That's how you need to approach salary negotiations. Wait for subtle clues or signs of interest that the employer wants to bring you on board. If they give indications that they are interested, then you can start talking turkey."

"What sort of signs should I be looking for?" I asked.

"They will ask you something like, 'Assuming we can make you an attractive offer, how does the job and challenge appeal to you?'"

"Got it. So, what could I say when we get to that point?"

"If you're talking face-to-face during an interview you could say something like, 'My salary requirements are open. I am more interested in the challenges and opportunities of this position. I expect that your company can pay a competitive rate.'"

"That sounds good."

"Yeah, but remember that if you're talking to a recruiter it's okay to reveal salary information. Recruiters are seeking 'perfect-fit' candidates. They need to know whether your salary expectations are in line with what those companies are offering. Most recruiters will not continue the conversation if you are not upfront about your current salary and expectations."

"OK..." I made a mental note to ask Emily about this. "So, if my research tells me I should negotiate for something higher, then what?"

"Glad you asked. It's a question that most people who *fail* never ask. Good for you."

"Thanks," I said.

"Here's what you do: frame any counter-offer requests in 'Employer-Focused' language. Avoid 'You-Focused' language. Remember what I said: It's not about what you want, need, or think you deserve; it's all about the value you bring to the company and what you will achieve for *them*. You need to speak in terms of the employer's best interests."

"Demonstrating Value," I said.

"Well put."

It felt good to know a few things, to be able to phrase something in a way that she had never heard before.

"Demonstrating Value, as you put it, applies very much to the negotiation process. Instead of saying, 'I really need more money because I have school loans to pay off,' you should say, 'I'm very interested in this position, but I must be honest that I am a little disappointed in the proposed salary. Fair market value indicates 18% more for a position with this level of responsibility, and 23% more for someone with my ability to contribute to your bottom line.'"

"Hell yeah," I said, very excited with how well she'd formed that sentence and hopeful that I'd be able to do it when the time came.

"Then, give them a few moments to bite their fingernails. After that, hit them with a question about how flexible they are with the offer. And if you can't negotiate base salary, which is common for some entry-level positions. You would also want to negotiate benefits."

"That's what I was discussing with my roommate about my last job offer. They gave me a pretty weak stipend."

"Well then, this is a good avenue for you. You should try to focus on alternate currency: benefits, vacation, etc. See what you get out of them. You may be pleasantly surprised."

"So instead of saying, 'I couldn't consider less than four weeks of vacation,' I could say, 'I realize you don't have any flexibility on the salary, but I wonder if you can consider an extra week of vacation?'"

"You've got it," said Elaine. She looked through the window and noticed that Robert and Bill were on their way up from the tennis courts. They approached the table. Robert bent over to check Elaine's ankle.

"How's it feel?" Robert asked.

"It's OK. We've been having a heck of a talk in here. I'm about to give Adrian my last two cents on salary negotiation."

"I thought that's what you called *me* for?" Robert laughed. He turned and looked in my direction.

I shrugged and pointed at Elaine, "She's the one who started it."

"She has a tendency to show me up," Robert said.

"Oh please..." Elaine pointed at her ankle. "I can't even get through a warm-up set without dropping dead."

"Honestly, it's probably a good thing you ended up telling him. I've always know that you're better at negotiating salaries. How many salaries do you think you negotiated in your entire career?"

Elaine eyed the ceiling, squinted her eyes, and counted by tapping her fingers on the tablecloth. "Fourteen, if I remember correctly."

Bill laughed heartily, still approaching the table. "FOURTEEN salary negotiations! I haven't even had four JOBS!" he joked. "Back in my day we only had one job—or maybe two, three tops. Let alone 14... The business world sure isn't what it used to be." He was still sweating, and was a bit out of breath from the last game. He wiped a towel across his forehead and looked down at Robert. "Is there a place to get a bottle of water around here?"

"Yeah," Robert said. "I need to get something to drink, also." He was still kneeling on the floor, studying her ankle with the greatest intensity. "Alright, Elaine, looks like you're going to be OK." He mocked himself, as though we were a medical professional. "I'm going to get a drink and cool off. This will give you some time to tell Adrian all those tricks you never tell me."

Elaine laughed. "You're not looking for a job, honey. I like to bestow my secrets on the promising youth."

Robert and Bill walked casually across the dining room and disappeared down the corridor.

"Where were we?" she asked.

"I don't remember…"

"Oh right, recognizing the salary." She sat up straighter in her chair and made eye contact with me. "Once you've come to terms with an acceptable salary, you should get the offer in writing. Draft and submit your own letter, outlining your understanding of the position. Make sure you evaluate your offers on multiple planes: salary, job duty, future potential, location, commute schedule, company culture, and so on."

"Why does the offer have to be written?"

"Because employers are human, and human beings are very capable of making false assumptions, or misinterpreting information. When you clearly outline your understanding of the points of the deal, you offer the employer a chance to clarify any points that you may have misunderstood. This will prevent you from making a horrible realization on day one at the job."

"Because after day one arrives, it's too late," I said.

"You got it. Unless you're willing to quit and begin the search all over again."

Bill and Robert returned to the table, carrying menus.

Elaine looked up at Bill and said, "Isn't that right, Bill?"

"What's that?"

"You should always get the job offer in writing when coming to terms in your salary negotiations."

"Oh yeah," Bill said with great conviction. "The pen is mightier than the mouth."

"I've never heard that before," Elaine said. "I like it…"

"When I was still working in venture capital, one of my mentors told me a set of rules. I've never forgotten these rules, and once I understood and applied them, it really made the difference for me in taking my success to the next level." He paused, taking a long sip of water.

PART FOUR

"**A**nd…" Elaine prodded.

"And what?" Bill asked.

"What were the rules?"

"Oh right, the rules… sorry, I'm getting a bit old, losing track of my own thoughts…" he laughed. I knew he hadn't lost track of anything, he was simply trying to arouse our curiosity. "The rules went like this… Rule 1: 'Business isn't fair, so don't expect it to be. If life was fair, we wouldn't be able to accelerate success.'"

Bill's voice was thick and commanding. I could discern a tone of great wisdom and worldly understanding whenever he spoke. His sentences were so chock full of information that wrapping my head around the true meaning of his words was, at first, difficult. In fact, at that very instant I found it almost impossible to decipher what he had told me. I had a moment of doubt that I would never understand his teaching because I was afraid to ask him for a deeper explanation. I thought it was one of those things I was just supposed to "get."

"Think about it," he continued, turning his palms up toward the ceiling. "As Americans, unfairness in business and life allows us to enjoy great comforts. If life were fair, hard-working individuals like you and me," he pointed at my chest then his, "would be living in the same squalor so prevalent in other nations. It's because life was unfair that our intelligent forefathers paved this road for us. Are you following me?"

Elaine looked at me. "Yeah, I do," I said. Honestly, I was a bit dumbfounded. I had never thought of my life in those terms.

"It's the same in corporate America," Bill continued. "No one gets paid what they're *really* worth. If you got paid what you were really worth, the company would not make a profit off of hiring you and the entire system would collapse."

I had never thought of this, either. "So, that's why it's so important to communicate your Return On Investment value on your résumé and during the interview."

"Exactly," Bill said.

"Another thing to think about," Robert interjected, "is that the ROI is important not only in the résumé and interview, but in the salary negotiation stage as well. Too often people go into a negotiation and say, 'Your offer is too low. I need $X amount a year in order to live...' This is incorrect, and will often result in the retraction of the employer's offer."

Bill looked at me. "You gotta speak to THEIR needs and communicate how much value you can generate for THEM. Say something like, 'As we discussed, I have the right skill set to make an immediate impact in this position, and I am confident in my ability to deliver 10% (or more) cost savings in the first year. This is based on my track record at Acme Corporation. Also, based on my contributions and what I understand to be fair market value for this type of position, a salary around $X amount would be more appropriate. How flexible are you with your offer?"

"Now I get it," I said. "This whole time, people have been explaining this stuff to me and I never really put it together until now. I see the whole picture for what it is: Businesses want to make profit off of their employees, and the best way to increase my chances of getting hired with a competitive salary is to demonstrate that I am one of those employees who can deliver profitable results."

"Bingo," Bill said. "Rule 2: Negotiating is about understanding the other person. My grandfather, when he first explained this to me, had a whole arsenal of insightful information, and the most important thing I remember is this: 'Whenever you're negotiating a deal, remember: If the other person is talking, you're winning. If you're talking, you're losing.'"

"That sounds pretty accurate," said Robert.

"I agree," Elaine confirmed. The vote was unanimous. I made a note to remember this point.

"Rule 3: Silence speaks volumes."

Each of us sat there, waiting for his next words, and wondering what to say in the interim. Was I supposed to say something? Had he asked me a question? What was happening?

After another moment I couldn't take it anymore. I spoke blindly, "Do you mean that I shouldn't always talk? Like I should create silence so that the interviewer feels compelled to say something and gives up more than they should?"

"It worked on you, didn't it? As soon as I stopped talking, you began to feel uncomfortable with the silence. You felt compelled to break the awkward tension that was created. You can often use this type of feeling to your advantage. Just remember: If things are going OK, but you want them to go better, give it a few seconds of silence and see what happens."

"Do you have a specific example? I'm not sure where I could apply this during my interview."

"That's a good question. Let me think…" Bill stroked his bottom lip and pondered.

Elaine spoke, "How about this: You're on the phone with your potential employer and they say, 'Our range for this position is $37-$42,000.' The first thing you should do is repeat the high number very thoughtfully and non-judgmentally."

"OK," I said.

"This is when you should stop talking and listen," Elaine said. "Bite your tongue, and force the employer to make the next move. Am I right, Bill?"

"Yep." Bill nodded his head approvingly.

Elaine continued, "During all of this, you should be establishing whether or not these numbers are Minimum, Reality, or Ideal. You remember that from earlier?" she asked.

I nodded.

Elaine continued, "Remember, the employer is now in a Buyer mentality. They don't want to lose you. If you don't jump at the offer immediately, it is very possible the hiring manager will come back with a higher figure. 'Well, I guess we can budget $44,000.' Without saying a word, you've just earned a 5% raise. But, if the employer does not respond with a new number, it's your turn to make a move."

"Wow, that's awesome. I'll definitely remember that."

"Yeah, that's pretty good," Bill said. "You should also remember that the other guy is trying to get the best deal he can, while still securing your employment. If he can get you for $41k instead of $44k, you bet your ass he's going to choose the lower number."

"That's why you can't have a scarcity mindset," Robert added. "You must communicate that no deal is absolutely OK." Bill nodded his head in approval.

"I always say negotiate with one hand on the door," Bill said.

"But times are tough. What if they retract their offer and I'm left without a job?" I asked.

"Fearing that the deal will run out is common. Scarcity is a negotiation tactic used all the time. Don't fear that the deal will go away over time. Remember: 'There will *always* be another offer down the road.'"

"That's so true," Elaine said. "When stores put something on sale, it's usually because they want to clear their shelves of all of last season's stuff. If their inventory still doesn't sell, they bump it down in price even further to get people to buy it. The same goes for employers."

"There's just so much stuff I need to consider. Potter & Sons wants a response by next Tuesday and I still don't know what to say. I have an interview with IWC but I really want to go for Empyrean, only Empyrean isn't a sure thing…"

"I know exactly what you mean, Adrian," Robert said. "I've been there before, and still get in similar situations. Don't stress out too much about your interview with *one* company. There will always be more chances to make a great career. In the meantime, you should ask Potter & Sons for an extension."

"Alright, I'll try that." I maintained eye contact with him and nodded appreciatively. Without people like Robert West, I don't know what I would have done…

Elaine shifted in her chair, and the ice pack fell onto the floor. Robert and I simultaneously reached for it, and I let him do the honors.

"How about you guys go back out there and play a few more sets? I'll sit on the balcony and get some sun," said Elaine.

Robert looked at Bill and me. "That sound good to you, fellas?"

"Sounds good to me," Bill and I agreed. We headed back out to the courts.

I had friends in high places; intelligent people were giving me the scoop on how to make a success of myself. I felt very privileged to be walking along those beautiful cobblestone sidewalks beside Robert and Bill. Maybe I would someday own a membership to a country club like this one…

When it was time to leave the club, Robert told Elaine to wait by the door of the dining room.

"I'll get the car and bring it around," he said kindly, pulling a chair behind her and sitting her down.

"I'll stay here," Bill said. "You know, just to make sure she doesn't try to get away." Bill laughed at Robert, who would now have to go out and get the car on his own.

"Yeah, she's been known to make some crazy escapes..." Robert joked.

I said my goodbyes to Bill and Elaine, and walked toward the parking lot with Robert. I finally felt as though the two of us had become friends. I was no longer some college kid was merely sharing advice with. I had shown my interest in his charity work by volunteering at least once every two weeks, and there was no question that he had taken note of my diligence.

I had to ask Robert something, and I had to do it now. I looked up at the blooming red bud trees and swallowed my nerves. It was the perfect time, probably the only time I would be alone with him for the next few weeks.

"So, Robert, I definitely appreciate all of your help and advice. I really can't tell you how much it's meant to have you as a friend and mentor." I wanted to ask him an important question, but I kept beating around the bush. "Um, do you think... uh... that it would be possible..." I cleared my throat and continued talking as if I was pulling off a Band-Aid, "Could I use you as a reference with IWC? And if I get an interview with Empyrean, could I use you there as well?"

He looked at me, a half-cracked grin shooting up the side of his face. Something told me he was going to agree. "Honestly, Adrian, I would be more than happy to be a reference. No question. Emily asked me the same thing when she started working with *Charity | Wells*. I can see why you two get along so well as roommates. You both think the same."

I couldn't help but smile with extreme relief. "Thanks, man," I said. "You've really taught me a lot. I'm really grateful. I don't think there's a way for me to repay you right now, but just know that I'll always remember what you've done for me."

"Ah, well, don't start tearing up or anything..." he joked. He patted me on the back and smiled. "It's been my pleasure. You should know by now that I love helping people."

"Yeah, I know. I'm just glad you decided to give me so much of your knowledge."

"Don't even think about it," he said. "Just get out there and *use* it."

He got into his car and I got into mine. Two different men, two different cars, two entirely different lifestyles, but at the end of the day we had the same mindset and the same desires. That, to me, was more important than anything.

*   *   *

The minute I walked into the apartment I emailed Potter & Sons and requested an extension. The hiring manager must've worked over the weekends or something because he replied to my email fairly quickly and granted me my extension.

I spent the rest of Saturday and Sunday preparing for my IWC interview, which was first thing Monday morning. I tried to remember everything Jamie had taught me, and I had created some killer SCARF stories to make my accomplishments really stand out. I needed to walk into that interview with an extreme level of confidence.

I pulled up to a sleek glass building. I was ready to do this thing.

I walked casually into the building and was escorted to a conference room that was bigger than the whole first floor of my house. Inside sat a younger guy, maybe in his late 20s to early 30s. He stood as I walked into the room.

"Adrian, hi! I'm Jordan Elbert. I'll be interviewing you today," he said, reaching to shake my hand.

I responded in a cordial fashion and the interview commenced, just as all of my previous interviews had. We talked a little bit about my background, and he gave me a bit of the company history. I already knew most of what he told me, thanks to the extensive research I had done.

Throughout the entire interview I made a conscious attempt to focus on my body language, sitting at 45-degree angles, mirroring many of the moves Jordan made, though making sure not to be too obvious about it. It felt a little awkward at first, but after a while I started doing it subconsciously.

After a barrage of questions, Jordan took a moment and looked down at my résumé. He finally looked up with an impressed look on his face, asking, "So, Adrian, tell me about the time you saved your company over a thousand dollars per year?"

I had prepared a SCARF story for this accomplishment, so it was fairly easy for me to respond. The words just spilled out of my mouth

First, I knew I had to establish the Situation: "At my previous job, one of my main responsibilities was to mail out letters of thanks to our customers every month. I did this in order to retain their patronage."

I checked his mood to see how responsive he was being, and I noticed I had made progress. He seemed to be engaged in the story. Now, I had to come up with the Challenge: "We had quite an extensive list of customers, so the process was rather time-consuming and tedious, often taking several days to complete."

Next, I needed to give my Action steps: "So, to avoid this mess, I decided to implement a new system by using the Mail Merge feature in Microsoft Word. I created a template thank you letter in Word and proceeded to enter all of our customers' information into an Excel spreadsheet. This allowed me to quickly personalize each thank you letter with a specific name and address."

"That was very resourceful of you," Jordan replied with a smile on his face.

I couldn't help but feel happy that an employer was noticing my resourcefulness.

I continued my story with the bottom line Results mixed in with some Naked Proof: "By using the Mail Merge, I saved my company eight hours of work every month for an entire year. Since I was paid $11 an hour (8 x $11 = $88/mo), I ended up saving them $88 a month, which, over the span of a year (12 months), accumulated to $1,056. My supervisor recognized my efforts and rewarded me with a $50 gift card to Best Buy."

Finally, to be certain I was on the right track, I needed to ask for Feedback. "Was that a sufficient explanation?"

"Yes, I think so... quite an impressive accomplishment. I know that if you achieved that here, we would be very happy."

Jordan wrapped up the interview by asking if I had any questions. I asked several company-related questions based on the research I had done and was surprised by how easy it was for Jordan to respond to them. He seemed ready for anything. I was well on my way to being able to do the same.

As I left the IWC building, I couldn't get Jordan's words out of my head. He would be "very happy if I achieved that here."

*   *   *

It was mid-week and I was taking out the recycling when I felt my cell phone vibrating in my pocket. At first I planned on dismissing it, but mo-

ments later I realized that this could be a horrible mistake. I dropped the recycling bin and pulled out my phone.

The number registered as UNKNOWN. I answered it anyway.

"Hello, Adrian Addler," I said.

"Mr. Addler, this is Jennifer Mansfield at Empyrean Corporation. I
am calling in regards to your recently submitted application… "

WE CANNOT CHOOSE OUR
EXTERNAL CIRCUMSTANCES,
BUT WE CAN ALWAYS CHOOSE
HOW WE RESPOND TO THEM.

....

—EPICTETUS
Greek Philosopher

CHAPTER 7

JUDGEMENT DAY

Sweat gushed like hot geysers of oil from my forehead. I charged upstairs, covering the mouthpiece to conceal my speed and clumsiness. I slipped inside my bedroom, closing the door gently behind me, and explained to Ms. Mansfield that I needed a few moments to prepare for our conversation. Jen was pretty nice about everything, and I knew that a few seconds' delay wouldn't sink the boat. In fact, this pause could have helped to make me seem a bit more professional, even more desirable.

I held the mouthpiece firmly between my thumb and forefinger and studied my Call Wall. An assembly of names, numbers, faxes, documents, etc. stared me in the face. Everything that I'd acquired during my job search was pinned to that wall for easy reference. I had experienced terrible moments in the past when, after answering a call, I had not been able to find the documents necessary to engage in an intelligent conversation. The Call Wall had solved this.

Jake told me it was a dumb idea. He asked why I didn't just put the stuff in a filing cabinet or a desk drawer. Once implemented, the Call Wall system is almost unbeatable for speed and visual reference.

The documents for Empyrean were right in front of me. I grabbed them off the wall, a few thumb tacks dropping carelessly to the floor, and turned to my desk. I slapped the papers down and took a seat.

"OK," I said. "Sorry about the delay, just wanted to get some paperwork in front of me."

"Absolutely," Jen said. "To start off, I have a few questions for you. This shouldn't take more than 15 to 20 minutes. Is that OK?"

"That's perfect," I said. I stood up and rechecked the Call Wall to make sure that I had all of the necessary documentation in front of me: résumé, Empyrean job description, research on Empyrean, list of questions to ask, and calendar.

I pressed the lock on my bedroom door and quickly slid back into the desk chair. I had established a perfect Quiet Zone, something that was essential for conducting a professional phone interview. Along with the Call Wall invention, I had realized the necessity for maintaining this perfectly silent environment, especially after Jake's unsavory slew of obscenities during my phone interview with Bauer Consulting Managers. I focused on my paperwork and got my head into the game.

Fifteen minutes of questions passed. So far, everything had been fairly straightforward and answerable. I could tell she was wrapping it up, and more than that I could tell that she liked my answers.

"So, Adrian, if we decided to hire you, when would you be available?"

I put aside my desires to take a post-graduation European vacation and said, "I'm ready to start immediately after graduation."

"Wonderful," she said. I could hear the keyboard typing something in the background. "There is always a ton of work to get accomplished around here, so being ready to jump in is crucial. We had this one guy recently who was going for a management position at our firm and he made it all the way to the final interview, which is a HUGE challenge in itself, and he told us that he wouldn't be available for three months! Can you believe it? No matter how bad it gets, people don't seem to understand that you have to make sacrifices in an economy like this one."

"It's true," I said. "You don't have to worry about that with me."

"Good. Needless to say, the other guy didn't get the job…"

I waited for her next question and she began, "Can you give me a recap of your past experiences in this field?"

I went over everything as planned. I told her about school, about my internship, and about why I was not continuing at my former company.

"I'm sorry about your internship," she said. "On the other hand, it will give you a chance to move to a better company."

"I agree."

She typed something else, and then, without any warning or indication, she fired the big question. "What are your salary requirements?"

I had been advised on how to respond, but somehow my brain hiccupped. It was harder than I had imagined to boldly maneuver around this question. I paused for a few moments and glanced at my Call Wall. I had several notes written there, and I quickly found the section on how to discuss salary. I took a breath and continued, "My salary requirements are negotiable. The money isn't nearly as important as the future opportunities at Empyrean. I'm sure that your company's compensation plans are competitive." I'd heard enough on several blog sites to understand that Empyrean would pay me well, no matter what.

"We certainly do pay competitive salaries," she said, formulating a game plan. I knew that my response had not been what she was looking for. She wanted me to give a number. "But, I have to ask you to at least give me a figure; that way we can see if you're in our price range."

"Sure, I understand. I'd be glad to discuss this information in a face-to-face interview." I smiled, the tone of my voice indicating to Jen that I knew she wanted this information, but that I would make her fight for it. According to Elaine, hiding salary requirements was standard practice... I hope she was right.

I kept in mind that if this final attempt to keep my numbers a secret didn't work, I'd need to be prepared to give my salary range, which was determined by my MRI numbers that I had come up with after I met with Elaine and Bill. I also needed to remember that I couldn't be too demanding. I wasn't exactly in a position to be calling the shots this early in the game.

Now it was time for the earthquake-inducing moment of silence. I let it roll. I let the silence overcome the phone line. I let everything cease, all words stopped, and I waited for her to make a move.

I heard her keyboard make a few clicks. Five seconds passed, which seemed like hours. Nothing... I debated saying something about the salary, perhaps trying to soften the mood. Then, at the last possible moment, I heard Jen take a breath as though she was going to begin speaking.

"Well, Adrian, you certainly drive a hard bargain. We always like that in a candidate. When will you be available to come in?"

I couldn't believe it. I had done it. I was moving to the second round of talks with Empyrean. We scheduled an interview for the following day at 9:20 a.m.

After I hung up the phone I re-pinned all of my documents to the Call Wall. I chuckled at the thumb tacks strewn all across the floor. I had been in such a hurry, and now that it was over I hardly remembered a thing. I had been trained so well that my mind must have reverted to auto-pilot mode during the conversation. Auto-pilot or whatever it was, it was working, and that was all that mattered.

*   *   *

I tapped on Emily's door. No answer. I cracked it, leaned my head inside far enough to take a good look around. She was taking a nap.

Too bad. I had to wake her up for this.

"HA!" I laughed triumphantly, exuberantly, and shook her bed, jostling her awake. "I got a callback from Empyrean!"

"What the hell is wrong with you!" She looked up with bleary eyes. Her expression suddenly changed. "Wait, what?"

"I just got a callback from Empyrean. I did a 10-minute phone interview and I have a face-to-face tomorrow at 9:20."

"Hell yeah!" she screamed, putting her hand up for a high five. "What's your plan?"

"Go in there tomorrow at 9:20 and ace the interview."

"You've got some stiff competition, I'm sure. Just remember that. Show those people that you're the man for the job."

"I AM the man for the job."

"I know, I know..." she said laughingly. "I just want you to be sure to communicate that to them."

I sat on the edge of her bed, staring into space, and imagined the interview.

"Alright, Adrian, get out of here so I can go back to sleep," she joked. "Congratulations on the callback. I'm really happy for you." She turned over and faced the wall, closing her eyes and sighing deeply.

"It's all thanks to your help, Emily. I can't thank you enough..."

"Oh, please... cut it out." Then, a few seconds later, she turned over. "I wouldn't stop looking for jobs just yet. Remember, you're up against some tough candidates. You're not the only one who really wants this job. Keep your options open and keep looking for jobs in your field."

"That's a good idea," I said. "At least it will keep me from having a scarcity mindset. And maybe it will keep me from sitting around daydreaming about the interview all day."

"Yeah, it's good to focus your energy somewhere else so that you're not oversaturated with ONE company."

"Thanks for all the advice," I said. I gently shut her door and returned to my room.

PART TWO

I sat around for the next few hours filtering through job postings. I found a few jobs that looked pretty good, and I adjusted my résumé to suit them. I was sending all of my information out via email. It was cheaper, companies like it, and it helped me manage my time. I put the names of each new company on my Call Wall and removed the names of several old ones.

I walked downstairs into the kitchen, satisfied with how many résumés I had sent out that morning.

"You decided to get out of bed today?" I asked.

"Hey, don't even start with me," Emily laughed. "I was up at 4 a.m. this morning running faxes for an overseas client. I have a right to take an hour nap."

"I guess so," I said. "What did you pick up?" I eyed the grocery bags. "Shoe polish? From the grocery store?"

"Yeah, you haven't heard?"

"No… What?"

"You put it on your hamburgers. It's like a marinade." She laughed at me.

"Whatever," I said. I took the polish out of the bag. "I didn't know girls used this stuff."

"From the looks of your shoes I assumed you didn't even know what it was."

"Well, I haven't ever used any…"

"I know. I got it for YOU. When you walked out of here the other morning I saw those scuff marks all over your dress shoes. You were in a hurry, so I didn't say anything."

"Thanks," I said. "How much do I owe you?"

"You don't owe me anything, silly," she laughed. "Tomorrow's your big interview. I'm trying to help you get ready. Speaking of getting ready, let's go to your closet and we'll plan what you're going to wear."

We walked up to my room and Emily searched through my clothes. "Alright, you should wear…" she dug around in the closet, pulling piles of clothes and boxes into the center of my bedroom floor. "This is REALLY a mess..."

"Sorry, I'm not used to other people digging around in my closet."

"Well, I'm making sure you get this job. One way or another." She pulled another box and leaned further into the closet. "Ah-ha! Wear this blue shirt! And where is that charcoal suit you bought last year?"

I reached into the closet. I remembered my mother telling me to buy a suit even though I had wanted to spend the money on other things. It was good that I had listened to her.

"How about this tie?" I said.

"That's what some people call a 'Power Tie.' It's red, it's big, and it's cocky. I've had tons of college guys come to interviews wearing these things. She studied the tie as though it was a dangling piece of seaweed. The last thing you want to do is come off as arrogant, because that's what the employer will assume. Either that or they'll assume that you're clueless."

"Wait a second... I see CEOs wearing red ties all the time. People don't think it's arrogant."

"You're absolutely right... if you're running a company! Adrian, just trust me; employers don't want to hire another 'Entitled Generation-Y Punk' (which is what they call us, by the way). Did you know they've actually written books about us as being 'The Dumbest Generation'? I'm not kidding you. That's actually the title of the book!"

"Wow... that's messed up," I said. I remembered learning about some sort of drama between Baby Boomers and Millennials, but I didn't think it was quite *that* bad. "But what if I just like the color red?"

"Forget your likes," she laughed. "It's time to make a good impression, not a personal fashion statement." She reached for a more modest but professional looking blue tie. "Wait," she said, snatching my belt out of my hand. "That's a BROWN belt."

"What's wrong with that?"

"You're wearing black shoes! You can't wear a brown belt with black shoes and a black suit!"

"It's not really that noticeable. Hell, I didn't even notice that the thing was brown. It looked black to me..."

"Men are crazy. The belt always has to match the shoes and the socks. It's either brown, brown, brown or black, black, black. You follow me?"

"I got it," I said. "I never paid that much attention before."

"Maybe that's one of the reasons you're unemployed," she joked.

I put on the suit and stared into the mirror. I looked pretty damn good.

"And please, Adrian, tell me that you're going to shave those sideburns."

"What? Why?"

"It looks ridiculous! You look like a Confederate soldier!" she said.

I laughed, recognizing a chance to one-up her. "Actually, General Sideburns was a Union general." Tenth-grade history class hadn't been a total bust...

"Whatever. It looks atrocious. Have you rehearsed the questions for the interview?"

"Yeah, a little," I said.

"If you need any help, just let me know." She took one last look at me. "Iron your shirt tonight and hang it out." She eyed me up and down two times. "You look good, Adrian. I'm really proud of you." With that, she left me in my room.

"Thanks, Emily!" I shouted through the wall.

I took off the suit and settled back at my desk. I took a few minutes to review my list of potential interview questions, aligning my SCARF stories with each question. After all the studying, I took a walk to clear my head. Tomorrow would be one of the most important mornings of my life.

*   *   *

The alarm cracked like a cannon and I turned over. I let it go off for a few seconds just to make sure that I was awake. Even after getting only six hours of sleep I was remarkably clearheaded and focused. I stood up and went into the bathroom. General Sideburns' impressive facial hair had to be removed from my cheeks, which I did very speedily. I also trimmed my nails and took a shower.

I got into the car at 8:19 a.m., leaving myself an entire hour to get to Empyrean. I merged onto the freeway and turned up the radio.

"Alright," I said to myself. "We're finally doing it. Just stay cool, calm, and collected." My old gym coach used to say that. He called it "The Three Cs." Funny how I still remembered it after all these years...

"Shit," I said, slamming on the brakes and bracing against the steering wheel. The car in front of me grinded to a complete stop. "What's going on?" I asked the other cars in traffic. I flipped the radio to AM 1140 and listened for an update.

"A four-car accident on the Southbound Freeway has traffic backed up for two miles heading into the city. It appears that no one has been injured, but vehicles remain on the road..." I slapped my hand on the wheel and looked behind me. People were putting on makeup, shaking their heads, calling their offices, standing outside of their cars to get a better view.

There was no way this could happen today. Not today. Of all the days there could be a massive backup... The digital clock ticked forward. Minute by minute. The radio droned and droned. The AC cut off and I was left sweating, a fly swooping through my open window and laughing viciously at my plight.

"Shit," I said, flipping open my cell phone. I dialed Empyrean and waited. Ringing... ringing...

"Empryean, this is Carrie speaking, how may I help you?"

"Hi, Carrie, this is Adrian Addler. Is Jen Mansfield available?"

The woman rustled her papers. "No, I'm sorry, she's in a meeting at the moment."

"I'm scheduled for an interview at 9:20 and I'm stuck in traffic. There's been an accident on the Southbound Freeway. I'm literally within eyeshot of your building, only about half a mile away, but the cars are gridlocked all the way to the exit."

"Thanks for the call. I'll let her know," the woman said.

We hung up. The woman probably thought I was a joke. Jen would probably scoff at this message, assuming that I was another hung-over college kid who couldn't get out of bed before 9 a.m.

My car was running hot and the AC was pumping hot air. I turned it all the way off and tapped my fingers on the dash. The man in the car beside me had fallen asleep. The woman behind me was laughing wildly on her cell phone. The entire world was seething beneath me, begging for me to move forward and make my interview on time. I laid my head back and closed my eyes.

My entire future was literally collapsing before me. I saw my life petering out into nothing. I felt like ramming my car through the middle of traffic, but I restrained myself. The work I had put in had been so extensive, and it was now being taken away because of this.

Why... why... why...

PART THREE

It was 9:25 when the first break in traffic occurred. I gunned it, shot through a small opening, and made the exit. I had been so close the entire time…

I sped down the cramped city blocks and turned into the office park. The parking lot was huge, and all of the visitors' spots were taken. I found the one remaining spot in the entire lot and parked. It was close to an eighth of a mile away from the building. Seriously.

I jogged across the pavement and burst into the building. There were floral arrangements and a black marble floor, and beside the main desk a giant man in a black suit stood with his arms crossed.

"Sign in please," he said.

"Thank you." I wrote my name and waited for him to open the glass doors. He did so very slowly and methodically, smiling at me as I breezed through. I boarded the elevator and realized that I had forgotten what floor they were on. It was suite 700, so I assumed that it was on the seventh floor. Yes… the seventh floor… I pushed the button.

Moments later the elevator stopped at the fifth floor. A chubby old man hobbled inside and pressed the button for floor six. Give me a break! WHY? Why couldn't he have taken the stairs?

I struggled to re-tuck my shirt and straighten my tie, checking myself in the brass walls of the elevator. The old man got off and I pressed the CLOSE DOOR button a million times as fast as I could.

The elevator lurched upward and opened, and I was suddenly face to face with two frosted glass doors. The name EMPYREAN was written in bold font and surrounding the name was the company's seal.

This was it. It reminded me of something from *Lord of the Rings*—something epic, with a great future, with unlimited potential. I took a deep breath and rolled my shoulders backward.

"People unconsciously grow tense," I said to myself. "And we must *consciously* relax." I closed my eyes and took another deep breath, inhaling for three seconds and exhaling slowly for six seconds. My heart slowed down gradually, and I regulated my breathing. The sweat around my neck cooled off, evaporated, and I regained my composure. I cracked the glass door and approached the receptionist's desk.

"Adrian?"

"How did you guess?" I joked. "I have an interview scheduled with Jen Mansfield at 9:20. I think I spoke to you on the phone earlier? Are you Carrie?" I made it a point to smile with my eyes and be extra friendly. Remembering Carrie's name and making a good impression might lead her to say something nice about me to the hiring team. You never know...

"Yes, I am Carrie. Nice to meet you. Please take a seat and someone will be with you shortly."

"Thanks," I said. I took a seat and waited. Several minutes later, Jen appeared from another doorway. She shook my hand and we exchanged a few words.

"I'm sorry about being late. There was an accident and I—"

"A few of our employees were late because of it," Jen said. "The important thing is that you called to let us know. That really helps." She extended her left hand, leading me into a boardroom.

"I'll let the rest of the team know you're here." She showed me to a chair and walked out of the room. I looked out of the gigantic floor-to-ceiling windows in amazement. The view of the city was perfect, almost breathtaking. Imagine working in a place like this every day...

Jen reentered the room. She was followed by two men with dark hair and glasses. They were at first very intimidating, the younger reminding me of Christian Bale from *American Psycho,* and the elder man, with his thick eyebrows and hardened expression, conjuring up images of George Clooney. I stood and shook hands with each of them. I was very conscious of my body language during all of this, remembering what Jamie had taught me at the bar about maintaining a confident pose.

"So, Adrian, tell us a little bit about yourself."

I had a flashback to my first interview with P&P. I couldn't wing it like that again. This one had to be stellar. I was no longer talking *at* the employer with the hopes that what I said would be interesting to them. Instead, I made sure to ask tons of questions so that I could formulate my stories to fit with what they were looking for. I also had to make my stories compelling by relating my experience back to how it would benefit the employer (i.e., saving time, money, resources, etc.).

I remembered how I had answered this question in my previous interviews with Potter & Sons, Farnam Brothers, and IWC. This time I had the skills and experience to deliver a perfect answer.

They seemed surprised at how smooth and professional my response was. They smiled as I related a brief history of my life, the trials and troubles, the successes and great accomplishments I'd made in the past few years.

Very quickly I summed up the atmosphere of the room, and using the Mirror-Matching techniques taught to me by Jamie, I made sure to match the voice tones and gestures of my interviewers. I remained business-like, thorough but concise, intelligent but humble, and aggressive but casual. In an effort to Mirror Match their postures, I rested my elbows casually on the arms of the chair and held my pen in my right hand as though I was always preparing to strike a note.

After half an hour of point-blank questioning, the table was turned. They opened the floor to me. I had remembered the Maverick Follow-up technique that I'd learned from Tammy Turner. I decided to follow it exactly, as I knew it would set me up for a killer conversation. I directed the first question at Jen: "Who would you point to as a top performer in the position I am applying for?"

After Jen answered, the other two men conferred with one another about existing employees, each man giving me a list of his ideas. It was informative for me, and it showed them that I really cared about being the best that I could be for the company.

The next step in the Maverick Follow-up was to ask about the key traits of these top-performing employees. The hiring team explained the traits in depth, which gave me great ammunition for displaying the same traits in myself in a follow-up letter, or in the next round of interviews.

"With the ideal employee in this position, what would you envision being accomplished?"

The younger man spoke: "An ideal employee would enhance relationships with customers and employees, would take control and display an attitude of leadership and a willingness to learn from their mistakes, as well as the teachings of others."

I nodded my head following his response; the older man gave me his theories behind an ideal employee's behavior. I made sure to take notes on each of their opinions so that I could differentiate.

It was then that I began formulating a story that would prove my attributes in these fields. I thought back briefly on my recent past, about how I'd come so far, so quickly. I would save this story, the story of who I really was, for the pivotal moment, delivering it when the pressure was on and letting my true colors shine through.

In my final question I was trying to advance myself to the next stage of the interview process. Addressing them all I asked, "What steps should we take to continue this conversation?"

I made sure not to be too pressing. I didn't want to come off like a used car salesman trying to force myself into the company. No one, especially a hiring team, likes to be pressured into a sale.

"Well, Adrian, give us a few days to go over the position, other candidates, and to discuss the current company needs, and we'll give you a call no later than Thursday."

"Sounds great," I said very enthusiastically, in the same breath asking for their contact information. (I needed the contact information to send personalized thank you notes.)

"We appreciate you coming on such short notice," Jen said. "And don't worry about being late; we're just glad that you called in advance to let us know."

"I appreciate that. Thanks for taking the time out of you schedules to speak with me. I hope to hear from you soon," I said, realizing that Jen was showing definite Signs of Interest by comforting me about being late.

"You'll hear from us no later than Thursday afternoon."

"I look forward to it."

Later that afternoon, when Emily came in from work, she was bounding with questions about the interview. She wanted to know how it went, what they said, if I had impressed them, and so on. I gave her the scoop, being sure to accurately recall the questions I had asked the hiring team.

"Good questions," she said. "You send them a thank you note hinting at your ability to display a few of those key traits?"

"Yeah, I sent them each a note. They're pretty good. You'd be proud."

"That's great. It sounds like you're on the right track. How do you think the interview went?"

I didn't know how to answer that question. I had been so "in the moment" that looking back seemed blurry and surreal.

"It went well," I said, still a bit nervous and unsure about what to expect as I continued forward.

* * *

It was Thursday, several days since the interview with Empyrean, but Empyrean wasn't the only job offer on my plate. Today, in addition to being the day Jen said she would call me back, was the day I was supposed to call Potter & Sons about my decision concerning their job offer. I didn't have an answer yet. I still needed more time. There were two rounds of interviews at Empyrean, and I wouldn't know if I got the job until the second round was completed.

The sad truth was this: Empyrean hadn't called me yet to ask if I would come in for a second interview.

I sat on the couch and stared into space. No TV. No music. Nothing. I waited for the phone to ring. I told myself that I would wait until 2 p.m. If I hadn't heard from Empyrean by that time, I would call Potter & Sons and accept the position. Hell, it wouldn't be that bad... at least I'd have a paying job. I was learning not to be too choosey ever since my dad lost his job.

At 1:50 p.m. my telephone rang: Empyrean.

"Adrian Addler," I stated in my most professional tone.

"Adrian, hi! It's Jen Mansfield from Empyrean. How are you?"

"Doing well," I said, eager to get straight to the point.

"Good. You really made a good impression on Tuesday. We'd like to bring you back in for a second round of interviews with Lloyd Brockelman, director, and Tom Yeats, senior director. Are you free next Tuesday at 11:00 a.m.?"

"Absolutely."

"Good! We'll see you then!"

"Thank you for calling me back," I said sincerely.

"My pleasure."

My excitement at having made it to the next round of interviews was slightly overshadowed by the fact that I had to call Potter & Sons to let them know that I was not going to be able to accept their offer. However, I kept telling myself it was for the best. Potter & Sons' offer was less than satisfactory, and their offices were in a pretty slummy part of town. I just knew there had to be *something* better out there for me. Despite all of this, I still had a hard time dialing the number. After all, I had never turned down a job offer before.

As it turned out, there wasn't as much to declining the offer as I had expected. It was as simple as saying, "I'm flattered that you think I'm the right person for the job, but I'm sorry… I won't be able to accept your offer. I'm pursuing another option at this time."

While saying this was a bit difficult for me (if you consider how long I'd been trying to find a job), it was necessary, and I knew it would lead me to a better deal in the future.

PART FOUR

I was killing time in my car, waiting for the right time to walk into the Empyrean building. My head was racing, sifting through a bunch of old facts and attempting to complete my last bit of mental preparation before the interview.

How had I made it this far? Past all the other competitors? Even with all of my training, this was something I had a hard time understanding. The thought of being at a second-round interview with Empyrean hit me like a tidal wave as I turned off the car. I looked into the rearview mirror, deep into my own eyes, and asked myself again, "How did I make it this far?"

It was simple. Empyrean had conducted a preliminary interview to get to me. They asked me questions that my résumé didn't answer, and they felt me out to see if they liked me as a person.

The people at Empyrean liked me. Good. Now what would happen?

Interviewing teams are notorious for saving all their tricks for the more important second interview. It's common knowledge that after you've proven to be a good cultural fit, you'll need to prove you can actually do the job. This is the main thrust behind the second interview.

By inviting you to interview again, the company is basically saying: "We are interested in hearing what you have done for other companies in the past, or what you are capable of doing for *us*." They like to hear SCARF stories (even though they won't tell you this, and hardly anyone gives good Naked Proof of *anything*, which is why so many people gripe about missing the job even after making it to the second round of interviewing). If (and only if) you've succeeded at demonstrating your value, that's when the fun really begins. Why? Because that's when they start to sell themselves to *you* instead of the other way around.

Through my research over spring break I discovered that there are very few *real* A-Players on the job hunt. Securing someone with A-Player attributes is extremely important to a company looking to fill a position. The last thing they want is to invest a lot of time and resources in recruiting an A-Player only to find out they lost the A-Player to another company. This is

/hy Potter & Sons had given me such a tight deadline: they didn't
.ve me time to find something better.

. was thinking about all of this as I was still parked outside of the
Emp,. .n office building. I straightened my tie in my car mirror and walked
a few paces toward the door. I had found a visitors' spot this time. Damn
right.

Strangely enough, I wasn't very nervous about this second interview anymore. I could handle myself around here. I was a qualified candidate, and above all, they liked me. What was there to fear?

The same man let me through the glass doors and into the elevator
area. I pressed the *up* button and boarded. The elevator doors opened and
once again I was faced with the frosted glass doors, the smell of fresh air,
and a great work environment. It would be a shame if they hired somebody
else...

I stood outside the doors for a second time, my heart no longer capable of slowing. I clinched my fists and relaxed them. This is how it felt to
come face to face with your dreams, your lifelong goals, everything you've
worked toward.

I was greeted by Jen and escorted down the hallway toward the
same conference room, surrounded by those same giant windows. I could
see from the hallway into the conference room, and seated at the table were
two of the most important men at Empyrean. I recognized them from the
company website:

Senior Director Tom Yeats and Director of Business Development
Lloyd Brockelman.

A lead weight dropped from my throat into my stomach, from my
stomach into my shoes. My feet were virtually glued to the floor, but somehow I kept moving and maintained my composure.

The men stood as Jen and I entered the room. They extended their
hands.

"How's it going. I'm Tom Yeats," said the gray-haired senior director.

"Adrian Addler," I said, constantly reminding myself to check my
posture and maintain appropriate eye contact.

"Lloyd Brockelman," the other said, outstretching his arm in my direction. "Take a seat and get comfortable."

"Thanks." I pulled out a chair and sat down on the opposite side of
the table. I leaned back gently, angling my body 45 degrees away from the

interviewers as a way of increasing my perceived value through my body language and not coming off as being desperate... even though I really was.

I was conscious of every little movement in the room, especially the relaxed shoulders of both men, totally calm about the proceedings, as though my interview was as routine as eating a bowl of cereal in the morning. Their calmness contributed to my ability to settle down a bit. I matched their postures, sure to maintain a confident and collected presence by keeping my back straight, shoulders rolled back, and chest out.

The men read over a few scattered pieces of paper, conferred, and suddenly I found myself under the microscope. The atmosphere changed from friendly to business-like, and the interview abruptly commenced.

"So, Adrian, what brings you to Empyrean?"

"I hear good things about the company. For one, I know that Empyrean is a growing force in the business world, and I know that working with Empyrean will provide me with a position with unending growth potential."

"That's accurate," Mr. Yeats laughed. He was definitely very confident in his company and in his ability to judge an interviewee. I could tell that he liked my answer by the way he laughed and looked at Mr. Brockelman.

"How many years of experience do you have in this field?"

"I have two years' experience working as an intern and am preparing to graduate college, where I have studied to eventually become an expert in this field."

"That's good," Mr. Yeats said, stroking his chin. He turned directly toward me, leaning his elbows on the table as though he was cutting right to the chase. "But, I've got to tell you, we've had a whole slew of guys just like you come in here and tell us the exact same things. Why should I hire YOU instead of them?"

I turned from 45 degrees and faced him straight on, mirroring his directive posture and meeting his eyes. I rested my forearms on the table and shook my head to let him know that I understood his conundrum and had an excellent answer. "What separates me from the pack is my ability to learn, to apply what I learn immediately, and to make the right choices under pressure. When you asked me at the beginning of this interview who I was... well... I didn't tell you the whole story."

I left a moment of silence to create suspense. Mr. Brockelman leaned in closer, as though he were huddling around a campfire to hear me speak.

"I started out looking for a job about four months ago when my supervisor at my internship told me that the company was downsizing and that they were canceling my job offer."

The men shook their heads.

"I started by sending out a bare-bones résumé and a cover letter that looked like something a third grader would write. Basically, I had no idea how to apply for a job. Like I said, I'm a bright guy, very quick to learn and apply skills, but no one had taught me how to do THIS." I pointed to the table, indicating that I was speaking about our interview. "I had great on-the-job skills from my internship, but I wasn't getting anywhere with FINDING a job.

"After a few failures I began searching for help. I found it first in my roommate, and then in a long list of other professionals, young and old, who were able to give me the wisdom and insight needed to take my job searching skills to the next level."

"So, you're not afraid to ask for help?" Mr. Brockelman asked. "Didn't it make you feel a bit foolish to ask someone how to do something that everyone is supposed to, well… know?"

"I'll be honest," I said, turning to face him instead of Mr. Yeats. "At times I felt a bit out of place attending $2,000 sales-training seminars and sitting on the back porch of million-dollar estates learning from one of the best marketers in the world. But, through it all, I kept my composure and kept my head in the game. Sometimes it takes a bit of fear to drive you outside of your comfort zone and propel you into the greatest decisions of your life—like applying to work for Empyrean."

They cracked a smile at the compliment.

"So, you got help from these people… then what?"

"I changed my tactics. I learned that I had to APPLY what they taught me, and that the biggest problem in most people's lives—including my own—was that we do not APPLY what we learn. Or, in many cases, we take far too long to apply it."

"I agree with that," Mr. Yeats said.

"I also realized that learning is a lifelong process. I can achieve so much more if I recognize the mistakes others have made and avoid them in my own life. The real-world wisdom I've received from my mentors is literally priceless."

"That's the truth," Mr. Yeats said. "I learned most of my business skills from a man who had never set foot in a college classroom. He is the man who founded the company that birthed Empyrean so many years ago. Luckily, this man was my mentor. He basically put me under his wing and gave me pointers on how to be a success in the business world. He introduced me to this industry and helped me to realize my goals. Speaking of this industry, what interests do you have in working specifically for our company?"

I nodded, agreeing that this was an important question, one that I'd given great thought to answering. "In the past few months I have re-realized my goals. You see, I had dreamed of working for Empyrean ever since I read your interview from several years ago in the *Tribune*." This comment made him sit back in his chair. He was obviously impressed with how thoroughly I'd researched their company. "The interview explained the kind of work you did and the kind of personality it takes to succeed at Empyrean. Once I read that, I realized how compatible and well-suited I was for this company. To put it bluntly, I was hooked."

"You're the first person who's brought that interview up in a while," Mr. Yeats said.

"Like I said, it was a big factor for me sending in my application. Aside from that, I had always imagined how great it would be to work for a company that shares the same values as me. I mean, you guys are very green, you donate to charities, you help the community, and I always thought we would be a perfect match. But, you know what? I had never thought it was possible because of how difficult it would be for me to get the job. I thought: 'Someone else will get that job… I'll probably be brushed over. It's impossible for a kid like me to compete with all the professionals in the job market today, especially with everyone being fired and laid off.'"

The men agreed. They seemed to understand exactly where I was coming from.

"I thought like this until I was taught how to take control of my own situation and become an A-Player in the professional world."

"Now that you're learning to become an A-Player, as you say, what makes you think you can fit at Empyrean?" Mr. Yeats asked. He continued, "Your résumé is impressive, and you obviously pay attention to detail. You're smart, you have people in high places vouching for you—I believe I saw a testimonial from Robert West?"

"Yes, Robert and I are friends. He's the marketer I was referring to earlier."

"That's great." He looked down at a sheet of paper, presumably my résumé. "All of this is definitely A-Player stuff. But, at the end of the day, what makes you the right person for Empyrean?"

This was the moment I had been waiting for throughout the entire interview. I had failed to use this analogy during my IWC interview, but I knew I had the perfect answer to this question. "Have you read my writing sample? I chose that sample for a very important reason, as it relates to my experiences."

"I haven't seen the sample," Yeats said.

"That's fine. I can explain it to you. Have you ever heard of the story of the Alaskan Black Wolf?"

Tom Yeats shook his head, smiling a bit. I could tell that it caught him off guard, but this is what I wanted. He was looking for a reason to lump me into the "everyone else" category, but this story would give him something to remember me by. It was a bit comical, sure, but I knew what I was doing... I hoped...

"Can't say I've heard of the Black Wolf," Mr. Yeats said suspiciously.

"I know it sounds a bit odd at first, but it will make sense in a minute."

"Go for it," he said.

"There was a breed of wolf called the Alaskan Black Wolf, and hundreds of years ago, right when the Black Wolf species was prospering, there was a horrible famine. To make a long story short, only one wolf had the strength and capability to go down the mountain to hunt."

The men hesitantly nodded. I could tell they thought I was stretching it...

"Now wait, just hear me out," I said, dispelling their early skepticism. "The lone wolf had never been hunting on his own. Few wolves have. So, he was understandably nervous. On his trip into the valley he noticed a Hawk, how it flew alone and watched the valley from high in the clouds. The Wolf tried to copy him. He climbed a rock and looked down into the valley, but his eyes couldn't see through the snow."

"Is this an old Indian story?" Mr. Brockelman joked.

"As a matter of fact, it is," I said. "So, the Wolf trekked down toward the valley, searching for the elk. He soon realized that there was no way to kill an elk on his own, in his weakened condition. The Wolf was just like me: very little money, no help, and an overwhelming task in front of him. You see, I should also explain that my father recently lost his job due to budgetary cutbacks, leaving me to pay my student loans as well as all of my bills. In short, I'm just like the Black Wolf: I had to grow up very fast and was sent on a mission to provide for myself as well as pick up the slack of the rest of my pack."

"Sorry to hear about your dad," Mr. Yeats said.

"It's OK," I assured him. "So, they sent me, the Black Wolf, who was very skilled and prepared by years of hunting with his pack, out into the valley alone. The Black Wolf kept watching the Hawk. How was the Hawk doing it? He could *fly*! He could *see* all the elk. Wolves notoriously hate asking others for help, but he did anyway because he knew that he *had to* succeed. So, he called up to the Hawk. The Hawk came down and the Wolf said, 'I am starving. I can't see the elk, but I know they're down there.' And the Hawk said, 'I am a bit hungry myself, and I can see the elk. They are in the far Eastern corner of the valley.'

"So together they traveled. 'I need help,' he told the Hawk. 'I can't bring down an elk on my own. Not when I'm this young and weak. Who could I ask for help?' On the way down the mountain the Hawk spied a den of Gray Wolves. 'I won't do it,' the Black Wolf said. 'I won't ask a Gray Wolf for help...' Slowly, however, he began to abandon his stubborn ways...

"The Black Wolf, realizing that he was left with no other options, leaned into the den, fearing that he may get his face bitten off. Inside the den there were two Gray Wolves. They looked up, rather uninterested, and said, 'Who are you?'

"The Black Wolf told them who he was, what his mission was, and asked if they could join together to achieve their similar goals. The Gray Wolves conferred amongst themselves. They needed help hunting, because even *two* starving wolves would have a hard time bringing down a healthy elk. 'But who are you?' they asked. 'We've had starving wolf after starving wolf come down this mountain asking for our help... what makes *you* so special?' And so the Black Wolf leaned in further, showing the hawk perched on his right shoulder."

I left a moment of silence, signaling that this moment in the interview was the exact moment in the story. I was looking for help in finding my food source (my career), and the Gray Wolves (Empyrean) were looking for help as well. I had attributes that none of the other candidates (the Hawk) had.

Mr. Brockelman leaned in even closer. "So… what did the wolves say?"

"Well, this is the point of the story where the Gray Wolves were left to make a decision. You gentleman, by the way, are the Gray Wolves. You're the elite, the ones everyone wants to work with, and I am the Black Wolf."

"And where is your Hawk?"

I pointed to my head. "The Hawk is more of a symbol I guess. My Hawk is my unwavering drive to learn, to see clearly through the problems that others cannot, and to quickly apply the lessons I've learned in a way that will benefit the entire organization.

"If you've read my résumé, I'm sure you're aware of the amount of *time* and *money* I've saved at my previous internship. Though my numbers pale in comparison to those of Empyrean's top performers, the mere fact that I'm able to produce results like these in such a short timeframe should indicate my high level of potential to this company. Also, I'm the strongest and most dedicated Black Wolf of them all. I'm the hungriest, I'm on my own, and frankly…" I took a breath, sizing up my next few sentences and checking their faces to make sure we were on the same page. "Making a career at Empyrean is not a want for me—sure, I *want* a job and career, I *want* health insurance, and I *want* to be financially stable… yeah, I want all of those things, but what I *need*, more than anything, is a position where I can bring my skills to their peak in order to help my team become the greatest success imaginable."

"Can you give me a few examples of these *skills*? In a nutshell, of course."

"I'm the kind of guy you send out on his own to fix things for the organization. I have great leadership skills and can adapt to new situations, as well as create new, more profitable processes for your company. This is evident based on the successes listed on my résumé. I also have a strong sense of vision—meaning that I know what I want to accomplish before I begin. For example, when I began my internship there was terrible clutter all over the office. People in my department were messy, scattered, and things were not running as efficiently as they could have been.

"One morning I came to work and found that our copy machine was stacked with empty coffee cups and crumby paper plates. It took me five minutes to throw everything away before making a copy, and I almost spilled coffee all over my reports. Being an intern, there was only so much I could do to change this. I had to get management involved, but I didn't want to come off like a snitch or a whiner. More importantly, I didn't want to be seen as a pushover for cleaning everything myself."

Yeats smiled. "So, Adrian, I'm interested in this. How do you achieve a clean office space if you're not the one in charge, you're not a complainer, and you're not, pardon my expression, the department's *bitch*?"

I laughed and raised my eyebrows, recalling the story vividly. "I wrote an email to my manager. The email explained, very casually, that I had seen a trail of ants running beneath a stack of papers and half-empty coffee cups near the new copy machine. I told him that they were beneath all of the clutter, and that I had cleaned up and they had quickly vanished."

"Had there really been ants?"

"Yes, I had seen several ants near the copy machine. Had I seen them that day? No. The important thing for me was that I knew about the company's strong policy *against* using pesticides. I figured that since we had gone green and didn't spray for ants, we had better take the necessary precautions to keep them out. If a little exaggeration would keep the ants away and get us organized at the same time, I was all for it."

"How did this guy respond to your email?"

"My manager instituted a cleanliness policy that was better than anything I could have dreamed. Not only was it easier for us to find materials, make copies, and organize our presentations, but we also made more money that quarter than in the past three. I can't say that this was all due to our cleanliness, but I can say that it speaks for my level of commitment to visions and goals."

"I agree. Sounds like great cleverness and ingenuity as well," Mr. Yeats said.

"Yes sir," I paused, eager to continue but wanting to collect my thoughts and give them time to form. "In addition to having clear foresight, I have an extremely high energy level. If we're working on a big project that requires extra time, I'll be there every second of every day. I'll work 60 hours a week if necessary, whatever it takes to ensure that the project remains on schedule. I'll do all of this because I enjoy it, and because it is the way I have always handled my life." There was a moment of silence, and then I came up with a zinger: "Relating this to the Black Wolf story: I'm the crucial set of teeth that your company has been missing."

The men sat quietly, their eyes cutting through my skin. I hoped that they were feeling good about all of this. Sure, the story had been a bit crazy, but it did exactly what I wanted it to do: It explained to them that, as well as being a lone wolf, I could learn from other people and ask for help. The story conveyed the point that Empyrean needed Adrian Addler as much as Adrian Addler needed Empyrean.

There were a few more questions. I steered away from the story, and the atmosphere in the room relaxed. The interview ended with a very positive vibe.

"I've got to tell you, Adrian," said Mr. Yeats. "I'm very impressed with your resolve. Our hiring team received your follow-up letters and I've heard great things about you from Carrie, our receptionist. We'll be in touch," he said with a genuine smile.

"And good wolf story," Mr. Brockelman commented, smiling and shaking my hand firmly. He put his hand on my shoulder as he escorted me to the door, and I sensed that maybe he'd been in my position before. "You've done a great job thus far. Keep your head up and stay original. I've never had anyone tell an Indian story during an interview before. That's one I'll remember for a long time."

"I hope it made sense," I said.

"It did," he nodded sincerely. "Talk to you soon."

I took the long walk down the hallway, finding it extremely difficult not to look back through the glass to see what Mr. Yeats and Mr. Brockelman were saying about me. I fought this urge so hard, so hard, but eventually I gave in and glanced through the giant windows. The men were smiling and shaking their heads in a manner that could be mistaken for nothing other than YES.

PART FIVE

A week had passed and my mind was still plagued by the Empyrean interview. Had I made a fool of myself, or had they really liked me? There was such a fine line...

I had continued applying to more companies, but none had so far piqued my interest. I found myself in economics class, Professor Hackmuth running his mouth full blast about statistics. Calloway, who was typically a few minutes late for class, swaggered through the door, his iPhone still in his palm. He snickered at something on the screen, pressed a few buttons, and put the phone away.

He looked right at me, nodded, and headed up the stairs toward where I was sitting. He took the seat directly behind mine, overtly winking at me on the way past and saying, "Addler, nice to see you," in a tone that reeked of arrogance.

Hackmuth kept speaking through all of this. I'm sure he didn't even notice Kyle coming in late because of his droning voice rolled on and on... "Research suggests that the percentage of annual revenue generate by the..." What was he saying? God knows I couldn't keep my head in the game. I tried to focus, tried to listen, but I couldn't take my mind off of the interview, my future plans, other jobs I had applied to, etc.

I had my eyes halfway shut, dreaming about something incredible, when my phone vibrated. It buzzed against my car keys, and several people surrounding me made sure to point their heads my way. Luckily, Hackmuth had his back turned. I silenced the call and pretended to focus on the lecture. I reached deftly into my pocket, removed the phone, and checked the caller ID. Damn it! Empyrean! Of all the times they could have called!

I hesitated, stuttered in my chair, and finally got the nerves to bolt out of the lecture hall. I jumped down 20 stairs as if there were three and charged out into the sunlight. I could hear behind me that Hackmuth had stopped talking. He must have been in shock, probably on the edge of fainting. No one dared to do so much as raise their hand in his class, much less vault 20 stairs and nearly break down the door.

I looked around to see if anyone was close by. I was alone on the sidewalk outside the lecture hall, and I opened my phone. "Adrian Addler," I said, covering the mouthpiece to silence my rapid breathing.

"Hello?" I asked. Nothing. I slapped the mouthpiece shut and cursed at the sidewalk. Of all the times... of all the classes to have to run out on... Hackmuth would probably fail me for this. Well, probably not, but I knew he would want to.

My phone buzzed again: new voicemail.

"One new message. To listen to your messages, press one—BEEP—First new message: 'Hi, Adrian, it's Jen Mansfield at Empyrean. Give me a call back when you get this. I need to speak with you—"

Hell yeah. This was it. I slapped the phone shut, flipped it open, and found Empyrean's number on my missed call list. I pressed SEND and put the phone against my ear.

"Hi, Empyrean, how may I help you?"

"Hi, is this Carrie?"

"Yes, it is."

"This is Adrian Addler. I was in about a week ago for an interview."

"Oh yeah, Adrian, I remember you! How are you?"

"I'm fine, thanks. I just missed a call from Jen Mansfield a second ago. I was wondering if you could connect me?"

"Sure can. Let me put you on hold for just one moment."

"Thanks."

OK... here we go... one foot in the door, and now it was time to seal the deal. All these painful weeks, months, years of preparation boiled down to today, to this very moment, to this very phone call where I would hear the good news that would change the course of my entire life. Describing the intense joy and anticipation within me would be virtually impossible. I was frantic, wired, unable to stop pacing the sidewalk in front of those old gray college buildings.

"Hello?"

"Hi, Jen, this is Adrian Addler. Sorry I missed your call."

"No problem, Adrian. How are you?"

"Doing well," I said. Enough with the BS, let's get this show on the road...

"Good, good. I wanted to discuss something with you over the phone, do you have a few minutes?"

"Sure. Go ahead."

"Well, Adrian, I've never seen a hiring team in such a quandary about who to hire. I personally like you a lot. Also, both of our project managers liked you, and the directors had many positive things to say."

"Great," I said.

"Your competition was very stiff, but your interviews were very impressive. We had over 200 people apply for this position, and you were able to make it to the final round. That alone is a great accomplishment," she paused. "However…"

I breathed deep. Waited. Why was she waiting? Was this an episode of *Who Wants to Be a Millionaire?* or was this the call telling me that I was hired?

Another few moments passed. Why was she stalling?

"However?" I asked, unable to take the suspense.

"I'm sorry Adrian, but one of your competitors had more experience at a similar position. He was a great A-Player, just like yourself—in all honesty, I think you did better—but his track record was too much for you to compete with."

"Right…" I said, sure to emphasize my displeasure with the decision.

I took the phone away from my face. I attempted to regulate my breathing. I hadn't felt so many raw emotions in probably two or three years. Jen's voice sounded like it was coming from 200 miles away. "Please don't be too hard on yourself. The young man who was hired is a whiz kid. He is about to graduate among the highest in his class, and is the president of his university's International Business Club. Heck, he's even captain of the crew team, which is something Tom Yeats was a part of during college."

Oh my God… This was not happening. This was definitely NOT happening. I couldn't believe it. I felt like I had just been mugged.

"I understand," I said, totally incapable of actually computing or "understanding" any information. I had simply not expected this. Sure, I had missed other jobs in the past, but this was Empyrean. This was the ONE… Not to mention that it had been stolen by Kyle Calloway, the biggest dickhead I'd ever met.

Not only had Kyle had sex with my mentor, cheated to get better grades than were even *possible*, cheated on his awesome girlfriend with a prissy sorority bitch, been literally HANDED everything in his life… he was now stealing my number-one job choice.

I almost punched the brick wall, but somehow contained myself.

Jen continued, "Before you go, I just wanted you to know that I thought you were such a good fit for the team that I tried to put together an opening for a new position for you."

"Really?" I didn't know that companies did things like that.

"Yes, and my recommendation made it all the way to the vice president of the company. In the end, he was unable to approve it due to budgetary reasons. It just didn't make sense financially. He wanted to hire you, but he didn't want to hire you now and lay you off in three months if we weren't able to continue getting contracts."

"I understand," I said, picturing Calloway picking his nose behind a giant black walnut desk, laughing and texting on his iPhone.

"Please, Adrian, don't be discouraged. You're a total A-Player. I KNOW that great things will happen for you."

"I appreciate it."

"I will keep my ears open for you, and if there's any way we can bring you on the team, I will do my best to make sure that it happens."

"Thanks for all of your help," I said, using my last bit of available energy to change my tone to sincerity. "It means a lot to me."

"Of course."

I wanted to hurl my phone into the fountain. I wanted to strangle Kyle Calloway. He probably cheated and got his rich old grandfather to get him the job. I remembered him from the Tammy Turner dinner. That old bastard probably had the entire city on some sort of payroll. I imagined Yeats and Calloway playing golf at some expensive course somewhere, each man laughing at my plight.

"That Addler kid… whew, he sure was fired up about working for us!" Yeats would say, driving one down the fairway. "But he certainly didn't have all the right *skills*, if you know what I mean…" (Pointing to his wallet and clearing his throat.)

Well, maybe nothing like this had happened, but for some reason that's what came into my head. I was experiencing such a tremendous shock that I wondered if I was sitting in an electric chair and Jen Mansfield had just flipped the switch.

I walked home alone, leaving my books in Hackmuth's lecture hall. I'd tell him I had a family emergency. That wasn't a lie. How was I going to pay my bills? My loans? How was I going to get a girlfriend, a house, a family if I was doomed to search in vain for the perfect job?

This was not the news I was hoping for. Not at all. I felt so hopeless, completely demoralized and unmotivated. I could have crawled into a hole and died.

A rush of voices exploded behind me and I looked back at the lecture hall. Class had let out. A tear formed at the corner of my eye. I shook my head roughly and turned away. I put one foot in front of the other and kept walking.

It was all a man could do.

IN EVERYONE'S LIFE, AT SOME
TIME, OUR INNER FIRE GOES
OUT. IT IS THEN BURST INTO
FLAME BY AN ENCOUNTER
WITH ANOTHER HUMAN
BEING. WE SHOULD ALL BE
THANKFUL FOR THOSE PEOPLE
WHO REKINDLE
THE INNER SPIRIT.

....

—ALBERT SCHWEITZER
1952 Nobel Peace Prize Winner

CHAPTER 8

VERDICT

I walked through the apartment, still in shock from the phone call. I headed past the living room where Josh and Emily were talking, and half-heartedly acknowledged them.

"Oh no," Emily said. "Adrian..." she stood to follow me, but I kept moving forward, floating up the stairs like a ghost and shutting my bedroom door. I fell face first onto my bed. The air felt hot, moist, and my forehead sweated continuously. I stood up, angry at the heat, and hurled my bag into the corner of the room. I almost tore off my shirt, taking only a few moments to undo the buttons.

I looked down at my phone, turned it off, and tossed it onto the nightstand. This was bullshit... This was total and complete bullshit.

A knock at my door. "What?" I said, annoyed with the entire world.

"Adrian, it's Emily."

"What do you want?"

"I want to talk to you."

She came in and sat down at the foot of my bed. I was shirtless and in a rage. I switched my khakis for a pair of athletic shorts. Emily looked away, raising her eyebrows about my mood.

"Look, I'm sorry," I began. "I'm not trying to be a jerk. I'm just..." I paused to get hold of my emotions. "I had a really tough phone call a minute ago."

"Things didn't go well with Empyrean?"

"You'll never believe what happened?"

"They picked somebody else?"

"It's a mistake you can relate to," I said.

"What do you mean?"

"They were sucked in by Kyle Calloway. He got the job over me. It's unreal."

Emily sighed and dropped her eyes to the floor. I could tell she didn't want to probe, but I knew that she was genuinely interested in knowing more.

"Ugh, are you sure it's him?"

"She said, 'Captain of the crew team and president of the International Business Club.' And, what's more, Kyle told me he was applying there. Who the hell else could it be?"

"That's seriously disturbing. He always was a smooth talker, though. Do you think he was capable of wowing them more than you?" she asked.

"I don't see how he could have been. I gave them everything I had. After I left the office, I saw the senior director smiling and nodding. I thought I was a damn shoo-in!"

"They had over 200 applicants, didn't they?" Emily asked.

"Yeah…"

"Nobody's a shoo-in with over 200 applicants. I don't care *who* you are."

"Well, either way, it's a damn tragedy. I'm sick of this shit. Bill was right; life isn't fair. In fact, what was I even thinking going for Empyrean? I was set up to fail from the very beginning!"

Emily put her hand on my back and tried to calm me down. "Don't be so hard on yourself. This wasn't your fault…"

"I know it wasn't my fault. The damn system is rigged! Kyle's grandfather probably bribed the president of the company or something… Fuck it. I'm going down to the coffee shop to get a job working for Paul. I'll sell pot for him on the side. It'll be great. No more applications, no more cover letters or résumés… just little bags of pot to sell to grungy underclassmen. Hell, I won't have to write ANYTHING!"

It was obvious that I was being sarcastic, but Emily shook her head with disgust.

"What are you talking about, Adrian? I've never heard you talk like this before."

"They ripped my guts out today, Emily. I'm not the same guy anymore. I left it all on the court, and Kyle mopped it up and threw it away."

"You're being dramatic. Cool it."

"Can you just give me a minute? Please?"

She stood up and prepared to leave. "Don't give up, Adrian." She pointed at my Call Wall. "There's a whole lot left to do. You've got a dozen other companies waiting to interview you. You'll get a job. Just keep try-ing."

"Oh, I know I'll get a job... working with Paul at the coffee shop."

"Would you cut it out!" Emily said sharply. "You better get your act together and stop pretending that this is the end of the world. You've come too far to even THINK about giving up."

"Whatever..."

"You should call Robert West. He'll have some good advice."

"I'm not 'calling' anyone or 'writing emails' to any more job-hunt demigods. I'm sick of this shit. I'm not cut out for this. I'm throwing in the towel. There are a million other people just like Kyle out there that are way more qualified for the jobs I'm applying for." I looked up at her, immediate-ly realizing my foolishness. I felt like such an idiot. Not because I didn't get the job or because I wasn't happy about my life, but because I was letting Emily down. I shook my head to ward off the emotions. "I'm sorry. I don't mean anything that I'm saying. I'm just stressed. I need some time alone."

"Call Robert," she said, gently closing the door. "Everyone's root-ing for you, Adrian. Don't let your friends and family down."

More pressure. Always more pressure. She meant well, but the weight had stacked like a ton of bricks on my shoulders. I sat down at my desk, shirtless and sweating, and opened my email. Junk... spam... trash... a forwarded message from Emily about saving the pandas... more junk... Robert West... spam... Wait? What? I reversed my eyes and reread the email address. Sure enough, it was Robert. I opened it.

Adrian, I got a phone call from Tom Yeats at Empyrean. He said he was thinking about hiring you and that you had put me down as a reference. We talked for a bit. I explained how I knew you, what I knew about you, eve-rything you've done for my charity, and he sounded interested. He said he had a few favorites, but that you were standing out among the crowd. Give me a call and let me know how it goes!
—Bob West

I turned on my cell phone, found his number, and dialed. I didn't give myself time to think; otherwise I knew I would have procrastinated.

"This is Robert West."

"Hey, Robert, it's Adrian."

"Hey, man," he said excitedly. "I hear you're in the final round of interviews at Empyrean?"

"Yeah, well... I *was*."

"And?"

"It didn't go as planned. There was another candidate... one of my classmates, actually. He bested me. I got the call this afternoon."

"You really wanted that job, didn't you?" Robert said somberly.

"Yeah. That was the plan. I'd wanted to work with that company ever since freshman year of college."

Robert remained quiet for a moment, presumably imagining what he would do in my position. "Don't give up," he said. "When Tom Yeats called me he sounded extremely interested in you."

"I don't know what else to do. A woman on the hiring team tried to create another position for me, but the vice president of Empyrean denied it due to budgetary reasons."

"Keep pushing."

"But how?"

"Adrian, if there's one thing I've learned, it's that it's never too late. Believe it or not, I haven't always been this fortunate. When you see me, I bet you think: Here's a rich man—a man with a great career, children who love him, and one of the best girlfriends on the planet." He snickered. "This isn't really the case. Let's rewind about 12 years, right about the time I dropped out of college. I wasn't a rich kid, I didn't have more than $300 to my name, and I didn't have any reason to wake up in the morning. Each night was a haze of drugs, alcohol, and debauchery. It seemed great to me."

What was he trying to say? I had no idea that this guy had such a strange past. How often did he reveal stuff like this? Surely it couldn't be good for business. Could it?

He continued, "After a while, my parents decided to cut me off. That $300 turned into *zilch* in about one week. They knew what I was doing, how I was spending my life, and they threatened to disown me. I was on the verge of homelessness, poverty, and isolation. Much to my chagrin, I was forced to get a job at a fast-food restaurant. Because I didn't want anyone from school to see me, I made sure to work the night shift. This way, all of my friends would come in too drunk to recognize my face flipping their burgers beneath the dim florescent lights."

"That's rough," I said, still unsure of where he was taking the conversation.

"Most nights I'd drink before I went to work. I'd wake up at 4 or 5 p.m. and go down to the liquor store for a fifth of rum and a gallon of OJ. I'd watch the sunset or listen to music while drinking and then walk two miles to work carrying a white Styrofoam cup. One night, my manager caught wind of my unsavory tendencies and fired me on the spot. I no longer had a job, which meant I had literally NO money."

"Damn… that's crazy. How did you get into marketing from there?" I asked, trying to decipher the true meaning behind all of this.

"It was a long road. I walked home from the restaurant, still drunk, and spent the night on the bare mattress in my one-room apartment. I was on all sorts of drugs at the time, everything from dope to speed, and I found it almost impossible to sleep. 'This isn't so bad,' I kept saying to myself, but beneath everything I was crushed. I had been fired from the fast-food restaurant. I was addicted to a million different substances. My life was entirely out of my immediate control. I was a worthless piece of shit."

"Minus the drugs and booze, this sounds like how I felt today."

"I'm sorry to hear that," Robert said.

"So, where did you go? What did you do?"

Robert took a breath, recalling a story that was painful for him to remember. "I knew I had one option left: my grandfather. My parents wouldn't have taken me back; my father was a total drunk and an asshole. I blamed him for all of my problems as a young man—and my friends were even bigger losers than I was. Some of them were living in their parents' basements; others were living in ramshackle apartments on skid row. I didn't want to fall into that category any further than I already had. So, I packed my things the next morning, left two half-empty fifths of rum in the cupboard, and drove down south to my grandfather's house."

"Was he a pretty understanding guy?" I started to realize that I wasn't in such a bad place compared with where Robert had been.

"Something like that… His parents came over from Czechoslovakia in the mid-1920s, while his mother was pregnant with him. They were lucky to survive the boat, but now that they were in America, they had to survive the streets."

"Man…"

"Yeah, I've heard too many stories to tell… Anyway, my grandfather grew up in poverty. He worked in the factories doing odd jobs when he was just eight years old. By 14 he had moved away from home and was traveling west with the trains, picking up odd jobs along the way and probably doing a number of things he'd never talk about. At age 16, he lied about his birthday and joined the army. While kids these days are shooting things in video games, my grandfather was parachuting into France, moving north-eastward into Germany, fighting for his life and the safety of the entire world.

"He was shot once in the arm but survived the war. After his service ended, he came home and finished his schooling, thanks to the G.I. Bill. During school he struggled to make ends meet, and afterwards he saved all of his money and opened a small diner. Over the years, he funneled all of his resources into his restaurant, expanding the menu and the facility, making it a respectable restaurant and not some greasy spoon. People liked my grand-father's restaurant so much that he was forced to open more locations. He had very gradually become the owner of a chain of profitable businesses."

"That sounds awesome," I said.

"It was pretty awesome. It was every man's dream: survive the war, come home, finish school, and make a successful company."

"And your grandfather did it."

"He certainly did." Robert paused, getting back on track with the story. "So, there I was: a 20-year old recovering alcoholic, jobless, a horri-ble record behind me, bitter toward the world, and I showed up on my grandfather's doorstep asking for help."

"What'd he say?"

"He asked me if I'd tried going sober. I said I hadn't, but that I'd left two fifths of rum in my apartment and I was never going back. I hadn't had a drink or taken any drugs in two days. I was pleased with myself. 'Two days?' the old man laughed. 'We'll see how you act after you haven't touched a beer for three weeks.'

"I told him that I was done with alcohol and everything else, that I wasn't going back to the gutter, and he agreed to help me... as long as I kept that attitude. I'm not going to lie, Adrian, I had a hard time staying straight. I screwed up a few times, dove back into the bottle, found myself sleeping on the sidewalk behind his house, all sorts of horrible stuff. One night, I came in drunk and I told him where I'd been. He looked at me with disgust and shook his head.

"'You're being a fool,' he said. 'You need to get your priorities straight. I had mine straightened out for me by zinging balls of metal and giant bombs. You'll have to straighten yours out on your own.'

"This made me really think about my grandfather's life and how easy I'd had it in comparison."

I asked Robert, "Did that make you want to quit drinking and get a job?"

"Yeah, I guess so. I wanted to quit, but the allure of that lifestyle was too much. It felt so good to sit around drunk all the time that I didn't want to move on. I felt security in the alcohol. It was something I could do very well, that didn't take practice, and that always worked 100%."

"You were afraid of trying to succeed in the real world because you thought you'd fail?" I asked.

"Right. I didn't know it, but I was afraid of the real world, and I didn't want to take responsibility for my actions. The alcohol was my shield against all of this. I kept trying to put that shield down and face the music, but times were tough for me. My grandfather came up to my room that night, took a seat on the edge of my bed, and told me something I'll never forget.

"He told me that there was one thing that sets all successful people apart from everybody else."

"What was it?"

"I'm going to explain that right now, but before I do, you need to listen to me very closely. See, I'm about to tell you something you've heard before. In fact, everybody has heard this before, but most people think it's too simple. They say, 'Yeah, yeah, I know... I know...' and they move on, looking for something bigger.

"These same people are the ones who waste hours, days, and weeks whining about how there are 'no jobs out there.' They're the people who consistently complain about being 'broke' or only having a couple bucks to their name, when what they should do is stop blaming the economy and take responsibility for their own lives."

"I was one of those guys," I said, remembering the times I'd complained about not having any money, or about not being recognized in my job interviews.

"Almost ALL of us were that guy... at one point or another. So, before I tell you what my grandfather taught me, I want you to make a commitment right now that you will follow his advice, no matter how simple it may be. After all, this one piece of advice is the single reason why I am the successful and happy person I am today."

I thought about it for a moment. "Fine," I said, wondering if I had just signed my life away on a wild goose chase.

"My grandfather said, 'NEVER GIVE UP.' He said it really hard, really strong, and with a bolt of lightening in his eyes that I'll never forget. In that instant, I saw all his years of poverty, the crackling explosions of bombs and bullets, the bottles, the broads, the endless stories he'd written in the wrinkles of his weathered face... I saw all of this emerge from the darkness in his pupils. He said it again: "NEVER GIVE UP."

I got an incredible image in my mind. I saw a man's entire life flash before me: the childhood poverty, the war, the hopeless desperation of looking for work as a young man. I saw it all and I cringed, but something caught fire in my soul. It burned throughout me, and I felt as though a fleet of warriors was standing behind me, ready to take on the world. I felt, at that moment, entirely invincible and in total control.

"Never give up..." I repeated, still in awe over the images playing in my head.

"My grandfather's exact words to me were this: 'If you really want to succeed, you'll never give up. You may try all the wrong ways, at all the wrong times, but you should never stop TRYING.'"

"I agree with that," I said. I felt my anger about Empyrean subsiding, and a new hope formed somewhere within me. Robert's story was giving me the confidence I needed to move forward with my life.

Robert continued, as passionate as an army commander, "Quitting means death, just like it did for my grandfather in World War II. Think about it: If you quit in the middle of a war, you'd not only be letting yourself down, you'd be letting down your entire country. It's similar with a job search: You wanted a job with Empyrean because you have a goal, a dream, ideas for the future. You believe that getting a job at Empyrean will help you make a difference in the world."

I nodded my head.

"Am I right?" he asked.

"Yes!" I yelled, a bit startled from the daydreams about my future.

"Well, let's make a loose analogy and say that looking for a job is like fighting a war. Quitting the job search would be like ramming your WWII bomber plane into Big Ben and flipping off Uncle Sam, all in one fell swoop."

We both laughed.

"All bullshit aside, there's one fact you can't ignore: There will be times when life is hard. You WILL fail at certain things. You'll send out a résumé, and it will bomb. It happens to all of us. Maybe you'll go on an interview and the employer won't like you or people will say you're inexperienced."

"Been there," I said.

"Life has seasons, just like the Earth. There's going to be springtime when things are going great and there's going to be wintertime just the same. These seasons also apply to your job search. And when your job search hits a winter season—which it almost always does—don't you dare quit.

"When people quit in their job search, or worse, 'settle' for a mediocre job, their dream dies. Most of these people end up sacrificing their lives in miserable circumstances that they HATE. They work themselves to the bone until they eventually get depressed, divorced, turn into an alcoholic, get addicted to something terrible, or lose their minds from resentment or boredom."

He gave me a few seconds to ponder that...

"So, I'll tell you again: quitting equals death."

I thought about it. I thought about the grandfather, and I thought about Robert West: two men who turned their lives around by following one piece of critical advice. Despite the simplicity, I could see the truth behind his words.

"So what happened to you? How did you turn your life around?"

"I listened to his advice. I threw away the booze, never set foot in the bar or the liquor store again, and realized that my failures and alcohol dependency were not my father's fault. I then devoted all the time and energy I had spent drinking and doing drugs to finding a job. After a while, I met a girl named Samantha, and we had children. She was respectable, not a piece of bar trash like I'd been dating all my life. I got promoted at work, moved up the ranks, and you know the rest of the story."

I found myself wondering what happened to Samantha. Neither Robert nor Emily had discussed her before. I wondered if Emily knew about her. Maybe it was better left unsaid.

"That's really interesting. I had no idea you'd been through something like that."

"Yeah... it's not something I like to brag about."

"My lips are sealed," I said. I was beginning to feel like there was a light at the end of the tunnel. "So, what do you think I should do? You got any advice about the Empyrean thing? You think I should keep looking for other jobs?"

"I think you've got to keep your head up and keep pushing. Call Tom Yeats or write him a letter. Hell, maybe you should charge into the office and speak to him in person. I don't know what to tell you. All I know is that a guy like you, with this much determination and drive, will make something of himself one way or the other."

"I hope so," I said. I heard someone talking in the background. They called Robert's name once, then again.

"Hey, Adrian, I gotta run… Call me and let me know how it goes."

"Thanks for everything, man."

"No problem. Hang in there."

PART TWO

I walked to the top of the stairs, leaned down, and called for Emily.

"What's up?" she asked, looking up the stairwell.

"I need your help." I nodded toward my room and headed that way, not giving her time to ask why I needed her.

"What's going on?" she asked, peering into my room hesitantly.

"I just got off the phone with Robert. He told me to keep moving forward, so that's what I'm going to do. I'm not giving up. I'm writing a letter to Tom Yeats."

"I TOLD you not to give up! Why didn't you listen to me in the first place!?! Well, who cares... I knew you'd come around. You want my help drafting the letter?"

"Yeah. I wanted you to give me some ideas."

"Well, first... hmm... you need to give exceptional examples of your character, aptitude, ROI, and desire to fill the position."

"Alright, that was my plan. I'm also going to use these notes." I pulled out my notes from the interview in which I wrote what each interviewer believed were the key traits of a successful employee. "I knew there was a reason I had saved all of this..." I remembered the Maverick Follow-up technique, how Tammy had said that one of the biggest factors was my ability to take notes.

I read down the page, Emily looking over my shoulder.

"That looks pretty good," she said.

"I hope so. Well, let me get working. I just wanted to make sure we were on the same page before I started running at full speed. I'll call you after I have something written. Would you read over it?"

"No, Adrian, I can't read over it."

I stared at her in question. "What? You wont?"

She laughed at me, "Of course I'll read over it, silly. I was messing with you." She headed toward the door, stopped, cocked her head sideways and asked, "What made you decide to keep trying? Ten minutes ago you were going to go work for Paul at the coffee shop, and now you're writing a letter to the senior director of Empyrean."

"It was Robert."

"Really? One guy was able to have that great of an impact? What did he tell you?" She was amazed that he had that type of power over me and she did not.

"He told me a really good personal story. It made me realize how small my obstacles are when compared with the ones that others have had to deal with. You should have been able to do the same thing. After all, you watch enough *Gossip Girl...*"

"Oh, shut up," she laughed, skipping down the stairs. I immediately began working on the letter, punching the keys decisively as I penned one of the most crucial documents of my life.

*   *   *

Four hours later, Emily and I completed the letter. Signed and sealed. She put her arm around me as I walked to the mailbox.

"Here goes," I said, shutting the flap and raising the red flag.

"You're the man."

"Let's hope so."

We paused on the far side of the street, our backs to the mailbox. We studied the trees, the freshly cut grass, and recalled our memories.

"You remember the time you forgot to put the brake on and your car rolled into the yard and smashed the neighbor's mailbox?" I asked.

"I was trying to have a positive, reflective moment," Emily said, laughing and retracing the car's path with her eyes.

"That's a positive memory for me," I joked. "I've never seen a guy get so pissed about a shitty, plastic mailbox."

"Tell me about it..." We shared another laugh just thinking about it.

We started back across the street.

"I hope Yeats reads this letter," I said. "It's such a long shot."

"So was being called to the final round of interviews; so was being *born*," she said. "Everything is a long shot, but you miss 100% of the shots you don't take."

"Good point," I said, recognizing the classic Wayne Gretzky quote.

Then I began to think about what she meant. Looking at the target... taking long shots... hmm... Where was my target? Sitting in the Empyrean office building. Why was this a long shot? Because I was sending him a letter from 15 miles away. How could I circumvent the long shot?

"That's it," I said, turning around in the middle of the road. A car honked at me, slowed to a stop. I waved my apologies and re-opened the mailbox. Emily waited on the other side of the street.

"Adrian... we've edited that thing 10 times. Please just SEND it and stop being overly critical."

"I'm not re-editing it," I said. "You said I had to take the long shots or there was no point in looking at the target. Well, I can't see the target from right here," I pointed to my location on the far side of the street. "And I'm not going to trust the mailman with the next 30 years of my life. Like Wayne said, if I don't take this shot myself, there's no way I'm ever going to score."

"So, you're going to take it down there personally?" she asked, surprised.

"You bet your ass I am."

*　　　*　　　*

I was moving at the speed of light, bursting into the office building and looking both ways for the security guard. He wasn't around. I eyed the glass partition, debated whether to climb it or slip beneath it by crawling on the floor.

I knelt down and checked the gap. No... it was too tight. I'd never make it all the way. The gap at the top was the same. I needed another way. I looked at the security desk, eyeing a roll of keys.

"Adrian?" a voice called from behind me. "Hey!"

"Hi, Carrie, how are you?"

"Good," I said. "I'm here to meet with Mr. Yeats."

"I didn't know there was another round of interviews?" she asked, somewhat suspicious.

"Well..." I checked over both shoulders for the security guard. "There isn't. I'm here to give him a letter." I held up the envelope as though it was as important as the Declaration of Independence.

"I see," she said excitedly. I hadn't expected her to understand, but she seemed very thrilled by the process of sneaking me upstairs.

We entered the elevator and made small talk. She wished me good luck, and I made a beeline past the front reception desk toward Mr. Yeats' personal secretary.

"Hi, I'm here to see Mr. Yeats."

He was in a meeting. Of course. Could I wait? Yes, I could wait all day if I had to. I was missing class, but so what? I could graduate, as long as I got something higher than a 2.9, which I could get without breaking a sweat for the rest of the year. It had certainly paid off to follow Emily's advice and study diligently at the beginning of the semester when things were less hectic. She had told me that finding a job would take a ton of my time, and boy was she right!

The secretary approached me after about an hour and a half. I thought she was going to ask for the fourth time if I wanted something to drink, but instead she led me to Mr. Yeats' office.

"Hello, Mr. Yeats," I said cordially, shaking his hand across the desk, an air of purpose and determination in my voice and posture. "I've brought you a letter concerning our last meeting. Do you have a moment to read it?"

He seemed a slight bit alarmed that I was in his office. Presumably, this had never happened to him before. "Frankly, I'm a bit blown away," he said. He certainly looked blown away, as though I'd come in there and socked him in the face. It wasn't a bad expression, just utter befuddlement. He had no idea how to handle the situation.

He opened the letter without speaking, read very cautiously, took a seat, and focused his eyes up at me. I remained standing, my hands gripping one another behind my back.

"You are persistent," he said, looking away and shaking his head.

My nerves reached a peak of near-explosive tension. I couldn't read him. What's worse, I don't think he had any idea what he was going to do. I put the Moment of Silence to work, forcing him to make a move.

"And on top of your persistence, you're a damn good fit for this company."

"Thank you," I said, my tone of voice implying that I expected him to say more.

"I'm busy today. I appreciate you bringing this in here." He held up the letter, still looking away in deep thought. He stood, walking toward the window and surveying the city skyline.

Finally, after several moments of this, he returned to his desk. He looked at me and nodded, as though he'd figured something out. "I hate to leave it at this, but I can't give you an answer right now. I have to make a few phone calls, try to pull a few strings. I'll be in touch with you soon."

"That sounds great," I said. "I'm very appreciative of anything you can do."

Mr. Yeats nodded his head and opened the door for me. "I've never seen so much persistence," Mr. Yeats said as I was leaving. Through it all, Mr. Yeats liked me and he knew how badly I wanted to work for his company. That was all that mattered.

Had I been too forward? Who could say? Perhaps. Then again, perhaps not. The people who are noticed are the people who break conventional tactics. I had certainly broken conventional tactics by sneaking into the office building and forcing a meeting with the senior director of a large and prestigious company. Would I be remembered? Yes. Would I get the job? Only time would tell.

PART THREE

The days passed and I found myself wondering where Mr. Yeats was in his decision, or who he was talking to about me. I spent considerable time guessing my chances of landing the job. I decided to temporarily stop job hunting in order to clear my head.

I was on the couch reading my economics textbook when Emily arrived home from work. She was sorting through the mail she had picked up on her way in. I paid no attention to her, as I was knee-deep in Diminishing Marginal Returns or some mumbo jumbo.

She approached me with an envelope. I grabbed it out of her hands. I looked at the return address and saw three letters: IWC. I tore the envelope open and unfolded the papers inside. I skimmed the letter and quickly discovered the verdict.

I had been offered a position. I couldn't believe it. There was even a personal note from Jordan Elbert telling me how impressed he was with my interview and that he hoped I would accept their offer "to work for such a prestigious company as International Western Consultation."

I couldn't believe what I was reading. The salary was decent, the perks were spectacular, and I would have plenty of room to grow in the company. However, through all of the excitement, I was still intent on hearing back from Empyrean before I made my final decision.

It became apparent to me that I could now "get a job" when I needed to. This part was no longer a challenge for me. My new challenge was getting the BEST job: Empyrean.

I set the envelope down. IWC was a good company, but it didn't help my mood to realize that I was settling for second best.

*   *   *

It was a Friday morning, two weeks since I'd talked to Tom Yeats, when my telephone rang. I was in the shower. Horrible timing as usual…

"Adrian Addler," I said, fishing my phone from my pants pocket, unsure whether the caller would still be on the other line.

"Adrian, this is Tom Yeats."

"Mr. Yeats, good to hear from you. How's it going?" I wrapped the towel around my waist.

"It's going well. I've got some news for you."

"Good news?" I asked.

"It may not be exactly what you want to hear…"

Great. Another let down. Here we go again. I started to slam my bathroom door behind me, but somehow kept myself under control and closed it gently. It was cold in the apartment, and I shivered shirtless while sitting at my desk.

"I made a few phone calls to our Denver, Dallas, and Albuquerque branches…"

"Yes?" I said, my foot thumping on the floor with anticipation.

"They were full. Not hiring for anything, not taking applications."

"Oh," I said. It was all I could mutter in the moment. I was about to say something else, but he continued.

"So, after that I went out on a limb and called Chicago. I talked to Steve Mintz, one of our lead hiring managers at corporate headquarters, and told him your story. I told him you wanted to work for Empyrean, that you'd starve on the street and die before you worked for any other company," he laughed. "Which is the impression I got when you busted in here last week."

"That's somewhat true," I said, laughing nervously and hoping that he was getting to something good.

"So, here's the deal: Mintz, who is a really nice guy, really eccentric but on top of his game, said he could use a guy like you at the Chicago branch."

"No shit!" I said, realizing only afterwards that I had just cursed in front of the senior director.

"Yeah. That's right. No shit. It requires a move to Chicago, and I know that's a bit of a stretch, but I told him I'd run it by you."

I looked around the apartment. It had been a fun town, a good four years, but the time was ripe for change. I waited a few seconds.

"You need some time to think it over?" Mr. Yeats asked.

"Yes, I'll need a short time to think it over before I can give a final answer."

"Let me call Mintz. He'll need to interview you first. I can set up a travel arrangement if you'd like. What days would be good for you?"

"Hmm…" I said. I was drawing a blank. My dreams were literally coming true, and my brain stalled while trying to find the correct answer. I couldn't believe that this was finally happening to me. It may have been a sign, a karmic reward from the keeper of the universe, or perhaps it was the well deserved payoff from my recent hard work. No matter, I still couldn't find the right words to answer Mr. Yeats' question.

"That's OK, Adrian. Just send me an email. The sooner the better."

PART FOUR

I conferred with Emily and Josh and they agreed that I should interview for the position. Though it was a long way away, I knew that I had to follow my instincts and take the job. Every second since the talk with Tom Yeats I had been high on life, incapable of being deterred from my ultimate goal. Reading a book, watching a movie, even walking down the street was almost impossible to do without thinking about Empyrean.

I flew to Chicago the following week and interviewed with Steven Mintz. He and I hit it off, and he sent me an email a few hours later telling me that I was hired.

Emily was ecstatic. She was a bit disappointed about me not finishing out the lease, but my moving out meant that Josh could move in. He needed a place starting next month and had no leads. This was perfect.

I walked upstairs and gave Robert West a call. I explained what had happened, how his advice had pushed me to make a move on Tom Yeats.

"I try to tell people: persistence is key. You were persistent and YOU got a job. Too often people give up or get lazy. I'm proud of you, man. You've come a long way."

"Thanks for being there to help me along," I said. "I hope things go well for you and Elaine."

"Give me a call sometime and let me know how things are progressing up north."

"Will do," I said.

We hung up, each man happy and satisfied that things had turned out the way we'd always wanted them to.

Jake came over and I told him the news.

"Let's go down to the bar," he said to me. "You guys want to come?" he asked Emily and Josh.

They looked at one another and nodded their heads. The four of us walked down the street.

"He just called you and said he had a position open in Chicago?" Jake held the door for me and I walked into the bar.

"Well, I had to basically break into his office and put a letter in front of his face before he was willing to call any other locations."

Jake laughed. "Leave it to you to do the craziest shit I've ever heard to get a job."

"Hey, man, I was scared at first, but I realized that you just have to go all out. I started seeing success as soon as I stepped outside of my comfort zone."

"I guess that's true. I remember when you told me about Suicide Calling or whatever... I thought you guys were nuts."

"That's what I'm saying. You've got to do whatever works, and that almost always means scrapping the old ways of finding a job and doing things you're not used to or that seem crazy at first."

"Yeah, I agree with that." He ordered up a pitcher of O'Dell's. We took seats at the bar, Jake and I, the pitcher between us. Emily sat to my right with a martini, and Josh was to her right with a gin and tonic.

The pitcher split into our glasses. Cool, frothy, dark amber. The best damn beer in the world was a victory beer, and here it was, my greatest achievement thus far: a job at Empyrean.

We drank the beers and ordered another pitcher. I got up to use the bathroom. On the way back from the bathroom I was bumped by a guy in a white collared shirt.

"Oh, sorry, man. I didn't... Adrian Addler? Is that you?"

Kyle Calloway squinted through the dark barroom.

"Hey, Kyle," I said.

"Hey! How's it going, bud? Weird to see you outside of class. You come here a lot?"

"No, not a lot," I replied. "I'm just here with a few friends. We're celebrating."

"Hell yeah. We're celebrating too," he pointed to several people standing around the pool table. "What's your occasion?"

"I just got a great offer from a company in Chicago. I'm going to move out there in a few weeks."

"That's great, Addler!" He laughed stupidly and patted my shoulder. He had a horrible habit of doing that, and I almost asked him never to do it again.

"Yeah, it's a great opportunity."

"Chicago, Chicago..." he mused, looking up into the ceiling like he was remembering something. "What's the name of the company?"

I knew that as soon as I said Empyrean his mouth would drop. He'd become like a wet fish, not knowing what to say, what to do, or where to go.

"I actually got a position at Empyrean's corporate headquarters in Chicago. I'm pretty excited. Don't know the Windy City all that well, but I'm anxious to see what's in store for me."

Kyle was beyond surprised. I enjoyed watching his face struggle to show a false sense of happiness for me. He searched frantically to find his next quavering, flimsy words.

"Uhhh, well, umm... maybe we'll be working together in the near future. I got a job at the... uh... local branch..."

I laughed, making fun of his position while leading him to believe that I was happy.

"Yeah, how about that. Maybe we *will* work together some day..." I hoped it wouldn't happen. I felt really good about myself, partly because, for the first time in my college career, I was on par with Kyle Calloway. We were two men on an even playing field. It felt good. I shook his hand, said my goodbyes, and returned to the bar.

"What took you so long?" Jake asked.

"Nothing." I sat back in my chair and eased into the beer.

Time was moving slowly, very easily, very calmly, and I felt like I no longer had anywhere to be other than Chicago. Did I need groceries? No. Did I need to go to the dentist? No. Did I need to wash my car? No. I needed to move to Chicago. That was it. Plain and simple. No obligations in the entire world besides my new career and this half-full glass of amber.

"Hey," Jake said, tapping me on the arm and pointing across the bar. "Check out the flock of chicks over there."

"Where?" I asked, turning very slowly, cautiously, as though this were the Old West. "Shit," I cursed, turning quickly toward the bar. "That's Isabelle... Damn it, what am I going to do?"

"Who is Isabelle?"

"She's this girl I keep running into. I always say I'm going to call her, but..."

"What the hell are you waiting for? If a girl like that gave me her number I'd be calling before I left the bar."

We laughed and slugged our beers. I was still overrun with indecision.

"I should just stay over here. After all, I'm leaving town. I'm going to Chicago! There's no point talking to her. It will only make me feel stupid."

"Oh, give me a BREAK!" He rolled his eyes. "Come on…"

I don't know what had gotten into me. A second ago I felt like a badass and now I felt like a frustrated chump. "Alright… hold on," I said. I collected my thoughts and gave myself a moment to think.

"Well…?" Jake asked impatiently. "Are you gonna go over there or not?"

"I've got an idea," I said. I turned and looked at Isabelle's group of friends. I searched their faces, hoping that I would recognize someone.

Emily leaned over to me. "I think I see someone that I recognize," she said, pointing through the mess of faces. "Don't you know him from flag football or something? Or the weight room?"

"Ah-HA!" I said, a conniving smile overtaking my face. "Yeah, I *do* know him. His name is Nathan Flowers." I turned back to Jake. "He was just talking to Isabelle and two of the other girls. We'll pretend we came over to talk to him! I'll introduce you two, and you can strike up a conversation, while I divert my attention to Isabelle. It's genius. Come on."

I pulled him off the stool.

"Jeez," Emily said, as I bumped into her while standing. "You've turned into a different person…" She was right. I was more eager than ever, stronger than ever, more confident than a raging bull. I charged across the bar with the pint glass and pitcher still in my hands.

"Well, if it isn't Nathan Flowers," I said. "I didn't know they let you out of the asylum this early?"

"They sent me out looking for you," Nate said. "It's been damn near a year…" we shook hands and talked.

"This is my buddy, Jake." I nodded for them to shake hands, and Isabelle watched interestedly, keeping her eyes away from mine. I could tell she wanted me to say something.

"These are some of my friends," Nathan said, introducing Jake and me around the circle of friends. When I got to Isabelle, Nate explained why they were at the bar. "Isabelle was accepted to the University of Chicago. She's getting her MBA."

"No shit," I said, still holding her hand, both of us mocking a first-time introduction. Jake stood beside me, hand outstretched and waiting to shake Isabelle's. He'd have to wait a long time…

I made it my priority to speak to her, actually cut between several of her friends, and started a conversation.

"Haven't heard from you in a while," she said. She tried to be perturbed by me, but smiled like a deviant when I looked her in the eye.

"I'm sorry… I've been job hunting for months on end."

"Find anything?"

"Actually I did. Today. That's why we came down to the bar."

"You always carry a pitcher of beer when you're trying to pick up girls?"

I looked at her glass, entirely empty, and dumped the remainder of the pitcher. "It comes in handy," I said.

She looked at the beer questionably, took a sip, and nodded her approval. "Good choice."

"I thought so." I cleared my throat, ready to give her the news. "I got a job working in Chicago for a company called Empyrean."

"Empyrean? Wow, they're pretty big-time, aren't they?"

"You could say that. I start next month."

"I'm moving to Chicago in three weeks," she said. "I'm going early to get familiar with the city before school starts."

"We should meet up," I said.

"I've heard *that* before…"

"I know, I know… I'm sorry. I was busy. I didn't have my head on straight. Can you find it in your heart to forgive me?" I gave her a playful smile. I must have had the glow of a confident man who had just gotten hired, because she seemed interested in me even though I had screwed up several times in the past.

I looked around the room, pretending that she was not the only thing I was thinking about. I felt like I was on fire, like the night, the bar, the whole world was MINE. I looked down at my legs and they were pointed 45-degrees away from her. I could tell by the way she leaned toward me that she was attracted to my indifference. I was still on autopilot and I didn't even realize it…

"I don't think I can forgive you just yet…" I could tell she was playing hard to get.

"What can I do to make it up to you?" I asked flirtatiously.

"You can buy me another drink. I'm not much of a beer girl."

"Sounds good to me," I said, and we began heading toward the bar. It was ridiculously crowded, and from behind me I heard Isabelle calling my name. She was trapped between a cluster of people, waving her hand so that I could see her. I pushed through the crowd while holding her hand and pulled her along.

I called to the bartender, ordered her a martini, myself another O'Dell's, and we snatched the only two empty stools in the house.

I found myself feeling very comfortable and contemplative, reflecting on all the things that made it possible for me to sit back and relax. All the teachers, all the weeks in the library researching, planning, burying myself in the anecdotes of others, everything had finally paid off.

The lights in the bar glowed and flickered. Isabelle's eyes met mine. The bartender slid the drinks between us and I slipped him a folded bill.

I leaned over and kissed her. No pretense, no words, just a gut instinct that it was the right time. I held my lips against hers. It was long, deep, meaningful, like a young man coming home from the war and meeting his girl on the dock.

It was the best damn day of my life.

Hands down.

CHAPTER 1 HIGHLIGHTS

Chapter 1 – Part 1:

- Your online presence is just as important as your physical presence. Make sure your online profiles give potential employers a clean and work-appropriate image of who you are.
- Your cover letter serves to promote you. Don't neglect it by putting 'generic' information. Make it personal and you'll stand out. Otherwise, the employer will think you're too lazy to write one or you have poor writing skills and can't write one. Both will rule you out.
- If you can't find the name of the department head you'd like to address your cover letter to, call them up and say to the receptionist, "Hi, I'm [Insert Name]. I'm writing a letter to the head of your 'whatever' department. Can I have the spelling of that person's name?'"
- When it comes to getting the job you want, you have to go out of your way to take the steps that will put you above the competition.
- Job-hunting is a skill. If you're not getting the results that you want, you need to change your overall approach.

Chapter 1 - Part 2:

- Interviewing is all about *perception*. Every little thing that you do during your job-hunt gives the employer a certain perception of you as a potential candidate.
- There are three types of people who apply for jobs: the '*Under Dogs*', the '*Smooth Talkers*', and the '*Stars*'. Aim to be a '*Star.*'
- There's no relationship between being "good" and getting hired.
- LinkedIn is a good way to research the companies you are applying for and to see what types of people they hire.
- Create a list of the top 20 companies you want to work for and practice interviewing with the bottom tier companies FIRST before pursuing your #1 choice.

Chapter 1 – Part 3:

- Hoovers.com is a great website for finding a company's locations, performance overview, press releases, and list of competitors.
- The key to being successful in the interview lies in your ability to be creative.
- Use Suicide Calling to get the inside dirt from prospective employers before you apply or right before your interview. It can only improve your chances of standing out.
- Make sure you always have a rebound plan, because plans like this will keep you away from the "scarcity mindset." People who are *too* desperate for a job repel more employers than bad breath.

Chapter 1 – Part 4:

- Understanding the rules of getting hired on an intellectual level is not enough to improve your current situation. You need to physically change your behavior and *take action* on what you've studied in order to achieve success in getting hired. Only then will true learning have taken place.
- Suicide Caller Script: When reading Chapter 1, did you stop to wonder *how* Emily was able to engage everyone at Proteus & Paulson? Did you wonder *why* John Mercer and Ken Barnes liked her and accepted her questions?

If so, the tactics and nuances behind her top secret Suicide Calling methods are explained, sentence by sentence, in a sample conversation below.

Incorporate the following into Your Suicide Caller Technique:

I recommend suicide calling several of your target company's competitors first, preferably before 8:30 a.m. or after 5:00 p.m. to reduce run-ins with receptionists and other gatekeepers. Have a single question in mind, one that you had researched but have been unable to answer yourself. Shoot for A-players, business owners, corporate executives, department heads, etc. and don't aim low to make it less frightening. Base your conversation with these people on the following sample:

Gatekeeper: This is P&P.

Emily: Hi, this is Emily Anderson calling for Ken Barnes please. *(Speaking casually and with confidence, surprisingly enough, will often get you connected to your target. "I'd like to speak with Mr./Ms. X, please," is a dead giveaway that you don't know the person you're calling for. If you want to increase your chances of getting through, ask for your target by first name only. "Hi, is Ken available?" Often times the Gatekeeper will assume you are a relative or personal friend. The bluff, however, is not fool proof. Sometimes you will get called out. If this happens, be flexible and never give up. Persistence is key.)*

Gatekeeper: May I ask what this is regarding?

Emily: Sure, I know this might sound a bit odd...

(When making unusual requests, use this type of lead. It will often incite curiosity, urging the person to listen before saying the usual "No.")

...I'm a Business major at the University and just read his interview in the Tribune.

(Tell them who you are and why you're calling. Try to play the sympathy card, "I've never done this before," or something the like. If something has recently happened in the media with the company, use it as a reason for your call.)

I've followed his career for some time now...

(Visit http://news.google.com and search for "First and Last Name." Find out what you can about the employer. You don't want to be caught on the spot without having done your research.)

...and I have finally built up the courage to call him for one specific piece of advice...

(Show your vulnerability. Make it clear that you're nervous and they'll lower their guard. I often do this even if I'm not nervous.)

...It wouldn't take more than two minutes of his time and I promise I wont waste a minute of it. Is there anyway you can help me get through to him?

(This wording here is CRUCIAL. You need to ask them to "help" you. Also, by saying you won't waste a minute of their time, you're cunningly excluding yourself from all of the other telemarketers and cold callers that actually do waste his time.)

Gatekeeper: Hmm... Just a second. (Two minutes pass).

He just walked in. Let me connect you. Good Luck. (Rings to another line)

Ken Barnes: Ken Barnes here, P&P.

Emily: Hi Mr. Barnes, my name is Emily Anderson. I know this might sound a bit odd but I'm a business major at the university and I've finally built up the courage to call you. I have wanted to ask you for one specific piece of advice for a long time and it shouldn't take more than two minutes of your time. I promise I wont waste a minute of it.
(Let the individual know that it won't take long. Basically you need to say the exact same thing that you said to the Gatekeeper earlier; just be sure to abbreviate it.)

Ken Barnes: Okay, go ahead. I have to be on a call in a few minutes.

Emily: Thank you so much. I'll make this quick. As the Vice President of P&P, as far as talent goes, you've probably hired some of the top performers in your industry, wouldn't you say?

(Listen to their response)

Who would you say, is the best [insert position] in the company? And how is their level of performance different from all the other [insert position]? Can you give me an example of something that this person does that other people don't?

Your goal is to get your target to stay on for as long as possible. If they are naturally a giving person and have an appointment that can be pushed back, they'll spend 10-20 minutes telling you their story – from which you can position yourself to ask more probing questions.

IMPORTANT: Start with big picture questions first then move into specifics. The tone of your voice is CRUCIAL in being able to pull this off. The more genuinely curious you are with asking, the better your results will be.

Examples: "How's business doing for you with the economy and everything? Were you hit pretty hard? Did you have to let a lot of people go? What kind of personality are you looking to hire? For what projects do you need people? How many people do you need? What association events would you join to start networking with some of the heavy hitters? Who are your best customers? Do you donate to any charities? What kind of software do you use? How do you do your scheduling? How do you stay on schedule?")

Emily: (At the very end of the call) Thank you so much for being so generous with your time.

CHAPTER 2 HIGHLIGHTS

Chapter 2 – Part 1:

- Though the job search process is quite a time-consuming undertaking, don't let it get in the way of your studies. Find the appropriate balance between schoolwork and job searching.
- The old adage, "It's not what you know, it's who you know," may be valid in certain contexts, but you still must prove to your employer that you are a driven and intelligent individual and will use everything your power to contribute to the betterment of the company.

Chapter 2 – Part 2:

- Don't be afraid to ask advice from people outside of your industry. Every piece of advice helps, though you may not think it applies directly to your job search.
- Mentors can prove to be beneficial in your job search, but they are only effective when they have eager and committed pupils.
- Your resume is typically the deciding factor for whether or not you are allowed an interview. Thus, it must accurately provide your interviewer with a snapshot of your accomplishments. It must also be visually pleasing so that your interviewer CONTINUES to look at it.
- To land an interview, you have to appeal to the employer's wants. Speak the employer's language by addressing the Three Pillars of Creating Key Contributions in your resume and cover letter:
  - Making money
  - Saving money
  - Saving time
- Money is the lifeblood of a company.
- Use the Check-Vibing Technique: Subconsciously tell your employer that your accomplishments are impressive by placing check marks next to them, rather than bullets. Check marks send positive vibes.
- Use the Naked Proof Technique: Quantify your accomplishments. The more numbers and figures you show on your resume, the more

your employers will be able to understand the true impact of your achievements.

Chapter 2 – Part 3:

- Constantly look for ways to differentiate yourself from your competition.
- Before submitting your resume, hang it on the wall and step away from it. Looking at it from a distance will allow you to decide if it is balanced on the page and if white space is used efficiently.
- Consider recording your interviews using a device such as TuneTalk, which plugs into your mp3 player. This will allow you to listen to your interview once it is finished and help you gauge in which areas of the process you need improvement.

Chapter 2 – Part 4:

- Consider volunteering. Not only are you doing something good for others or your community, you're also adding valuable work experience to your resume. Employers like to see proactive candidates.
- Treat each new experience as an opportunity to network. You never know whom you may meet or what they may be able to do for you.

Chapter 2 – Part 5:

- If you feel uneasy during an interview, your interviewer will pick up on it. Remain confident throughout the entire process.
- Remember that you won't just be asked behavioral-based questions about your previous work experience. You may be asked much simpler questions, such as, "What interests you about this field?" Though these questions may seem easy to answer, it may prove to be incredibly difficult to respond to them. Be sure to rehearse questions such as these prior to the interview.
- During the interview you will be asked several questions. You will also have an opportunity to ask your own questions, so do it! Be sure not to ruin an opportunity to learn more about the company and to show your interest in the position.

CHAPTER 3 HIGHLIGHTS

Chapter 3 – Part 1:

- Phone interviews are typically the initial step of the interview process. During a phone interview, be sure to eliminate any possible distractions that may hinder your interview performance.

Chapter 3 – Part 2:

- Do not let rejection letters diminish your motivation. Rather, see each rejection letter as a learning opportunity, a chance to improve your interviewing skills.

- Perform vision exercises to discover the best way to fulfill your goals. Start with the big picture item (i.e. be financially secure), and continually probe with questions until you discover exactly how you are going to achieve that goal. Clear visions create causes. You have to visualize what you want before you can actually achieve it.

Chapter 3 – Part 3:

- Testimonials are one of the job seeker's greatest weapons. They instill trust in weary hiring managers. When they see former supervisors, community leaders, professors, and peers saying good things about you, their natural tendencies are to find you trustworthy. You have people who can vouch for your accomplishments.

- If you have several testimonials, it is best to use only those written by people in high management positions.

- Think of the hiring process as a chance to market or advertise your talents. Marketers use newspapers, magazines, online ads, etc. to market their goods. Job seekers use their resumes and cover letters for the same purpose.

- Old marketing strategies involved a push strategy, which is to say that companies simply put their names out there and waited for customers to come to them. This is the conventional advertising strategy. The more efficient means of advertising is the pull strategy, which allows companies to attract customers to them, rather than having to reach out to customers.

- This pull strategy can also be implemented during the interviewing process. The idea behind "getting THEIR perspective in HERE" is that by understanding exactly what the employer wants, job seekers are able to customize their resumes and cover letters to employers' specifications. This puts those job candidates at a competitive advantage, as they already know exactly what the employer is looking for.

- It's not about how many interviews you go on, but the quality of your interviewing skill that determines your likelihood of being successful with landing more interviews or getting hired.

- There are two mindsets when it comes to the hiring process, that of the hiring manager and that of the job seeker. These perspectives are complete opposites of one another. The mindset of the hiring manager is to get the most work out of an employee, while spending the least amount of money. The mindset of the average job seeker is to find the highest-paying job that requires the least amount of work. You need to understand what the hiring manager is looking for in an employee, while also making sure you're getting a fair deal.

- Rapid Implementation is the distance between the time you hear and learn something and the time you put it into action. The less amount of time this takes, the better.

CHAPTER 4 HIGHLIGHTS

Chapter 4 – Part 1:

- Always follow up an interview or counseling session with a personalized "thank you" card. It is proper business etiquette. This can be done through email, but postal delivery is preferable. The more you communicate with employers, the more likely they are to remember you, and the better your chances of getting ahead.
- Never miss an opportunity to improve your speed of implementation. Consider reading books on hiring techniques to get a better understanding of how employers think during the interview process. These books will offer you insider information, and will greatly increase your speed of implementation

Chapter 4 – Part 2:

- If not already, become comfortable communicating… and communicating well. Eighty percent of your day is spent communicating, whether verbally, virtually, or kinesthetically.
- People decide whether or not they like you based on limited interaction. A woman will typically determine whether or not she likes you in about 15 seconds. Men are a little more generous. They give you 35 to 40 seconds before they decide.
- On average, you have 5.3 minutes to make a good first impression. If you have not done so by this point, there is little hope that you will be able to sway your interviewer's opinion.

Chapter 4 – Part 3:

- The best time to schedule an interview is in the morning. Why?
  - By 11:00 a.m., people start thinking about lunch.
  - By 12:00 a.m., people are either eating or on their way to lunch.
  - By 1:00 p.m., people get tired due to physiological responses to a meal.
  - By 3:00 p.m., people are thinking of going home, not to mention they are tired.

- Employers want 'A Players.' An 'A Player' is someone who finds ways to get the job done in *less time* with *less cost*. The more value you're able to demonstrate as an 'A Player,' the more attractive you'll look as a candidate. The trick is demonstrating that YOU have higher value than your competition.

- Human minds have an easier time understanding something in relation to a story, rather than stated facts. Stories cut through all of the skepticism, suspicion, and psychological defense mechanisms that people have when they don't know you. This is also the reason why we have organized our book in this way.

- By intentionally emphasizing the elements of your work experience that are very compelling, you design a story that helps a prospective employer get to know you, relate to you, build trust with you, and that also frames you in the right light.

- Be on the lookout for employers' Signs of Interest, or SOIs. These can include: leaning forward while you are speaking, offering compliments on your achievements, asking you several questions about your accomplishments, and even salary negotiations during the early phases of the interview process.

- The three most important attributes of an 'A-Player' as it applies to the interview:
  - **Psychological Mindset**: An A-PLAYER makes the correct decisions and performs well under extreme situations, intense stress, extra hours, and does so with the greatest consistency while yielding the most positive results.
  - **Good Listening Skills**: A-PLAYERS always "lead with their ears" at all stages in their career. You must identify people's wants and act accordingly to engage them and fulfill those wants.
  - **Storytelling Skills**: Important not only in the interview, you must remember to use SCARF stories and precise, intelligent, confident powers of speech to deliver your point expressly to the ears of your interviewer.

- The S.C.A.R.F. Technique should be used to formulate success stories about your accomplishments:
  - S—Setting: Where the story took place.
  - C—Challenge: What specific situation were you faced with?

- o A—Action: What specific action did you take to complete the task?
- o R—Result: What were the bottom line results?
- o F—Feedback: Ask the interviewer a question to see if you are on the right track.

- If, at the end of the interview, you cannot think of a question to ask your interviewer, rely on the Maverick Follow-Up Technique. To prove to your interviewer that you want to be a valued member of their staff, you have to get an idea of what their top players are like. This technique consists of three questions:
  - o *"Out of your current employees, who would you choose as the top performer in this position?"* This allows them to look at their staff and decide who their A, B, and C Players are."
  - o *"What traits make him or her stand out?"* By asking this question, you are able to compare your traits to those of the company's A Players.
  - o *"What specific actions or behaviors make him or her so successful?"* Asking this allows you to gauge how your actions and behaviors stack up next to those of someone who has experience in your field. If you can demonstrate that you have the potential to be an 'A-Player,' your chances of landing the job are much higher.

Chapter 5 Highlights

Chapter 5 – Part 1:
- Shed your *employee*-focused approach to getting hired and rewire yourself to becoming *employer*-focused. In order to do this, you need to continually train yourself to think like the employer you are aiming to be hired by.
- Mis-hiring is a mistake all companies try to avoid. It costs companies who mis-hire employees 14.2 times the salary of that individual, after you factor in all of the HR costs, recruiting costs, executive management, severance packages, etc.
- Building a cohesive team translates into big bucks for a company. The challenge with this, however, is overcoming the human behavioral tendencies known to corrupt teams:
  - Absence of trust
  - Fear of conflict
  - Lack of commitment
  - Avoidance of accountability
  - Inattention to results

Chapter 5 – Part 2:
- Patrick Lenconi outlines, in his book, *Three Signs of a Miserable Job*, "the three key principles that make work miserable:"
  - Irrelevance
  - Immeasurability
  - Anonymity

  Make sure to watch for these signs during job interviews.

Chapter 5 – Part 3:
- Major events may occur in life that seem like dead ends, such as the laying off of a parent or a death in the family, but don't treat them as such. Instead, treat them as motivational devices that make you work even harder to achieve your goal.
- Stress not only takes a toll on you emotionally and mentally, but also physically. When stressed, we tend to stiffen our muscles and look uptight or uncomfortable.

- Stress is a *subconscious* phenomenon. We do not know we are stressing ourselves out, but we do know when we are stressed. The best way to relieve this stress is by *consciously* relaxing, using the Anxiety Annihilator Technique. To achieve stress-relief properly, plant your feet on the floor, inhale through your nose for three seconds, and exhale through your mouth for six. Continue this cycle until you feel relaxed.
- The trick to any successful interaction is knowing how to display confident body language. In addition to this, you must be able to read body language accurately.
- Women are ten times more perceptive of body language than men.
- Confidence and composure are signs of higher status, and the majority of people are pre-wired to be attracted to high status.

Chapter 5 – Part 4:

- Interviewers begin to evaluate credibility within the first seven seconds of walking in the door. They do this based on clothes. Ninety percent of their opinion will be made in the first five minutes, and 60-80% of the impact you make is non-verbal.
- Women will look at male candidate's hair length, clothes design, color coordination, the creases in trousers, shine on shoes, and the dimple in the tie.
- Male interviewers will check out the chest, legs, and butt of female candidates.
- Male interviewers will only check the shine of another man's shoes and the dimple in the tie.
- Exhibit confidence by lifting your chest, putting your shoulders back, tilting your head back, projecting yourself, and, above all, maintaining eye contact. Be careful not to overdo it, though. Make sure you still feel comfortable.
- The Mirroring-Matching Technique, in which you subtly mimic your interviewer's movements, is another great way to build rapport. The more you are able to imitate the behaviors and mannerisms of your interviewer, the more comfortable he or she will become with you and the more you will be seen as a peer, rather than a candidate.

- Common signs of disinterest: sitting at a 45-degree angle away from the other person, sitting with legs crossed, and smiling with your mouth, instead of with your eyes.
- In an interview, when you sit at a 45-degree angle, you subconsciously increase your perceived value to whomever you're speaking with, because they haven't won your approval yet.

CHAPTER 6 HIGHLIGHTS

Chapter 6 – Part 1:

- When a company asks for a writing sample, don't stress yourself out by creating something off the top of your head. Instead, use something you know is well written, such as a term paper that received a good grade in a class. Often, these will be saved on your hard drive, so there's no need to retype them.

Chapter 6 – Part 2:

- If you receive an offer, but are not satisfied with the compensation package, don't be afraid to negotiate. In fact, it's common practice to negotiate salaries. If a company is inflexible with the salary, consider asking for more perks and benefits.
- 57% of men negotiate for higher salaries, while only 7% of women negotiate.
- A lower starting salary translates to slower growth UP the pay scale.
- Most employers expect you to negotiate. To do so, you must first calculate your Fair Market Value, or FMV. This is a dollar amount that details how much you are worth to an employer, based on your industry and location. Websites such as Salary.com are great tools to use when calculating your Fair Market Value.
- Your negotiating strength is dependent on the amount of demand for your skills. This follows the Law of Supply and Demand. When supply is low, demand is high, which leads to greater negotiating strength.
- Come up with your M.R.I. numbers prior to your interview.
  - M—Minimum: The lowest salary you will accept.
  - R—Realistic: The amount you can accept and feel adequately compensated.
  - I—Ideal: The amount you would need to live very comfortably.
- Delay any money talk until the interviewer has shifted from Shopper to Buyer. Look for Signs of Interest to know when this shift occurs.

- Once you receive an offer, make sure you get it in writing. Relying on verbal pacts can be dangerous, as people often forget what was agreed upon.
- Remember the three rules of salary negotiation:
    - **Business is never fair, so don't expect it to be.** No one gets paid what they are *really* worth. That's why it's important to emphasize your Return on Investment value in your resume and during the interview.
    - **Negotiation is about understanding the other person.** If your interviewer is talking, you are winning. If you are doing all of the talking, you are losing.
    - **Silence speaks volumes.** If things are going well, but you want them to go better, give it a few seconds of silence and see what happens.
- When an employer states a salary range, sit back, repeat the higher figure, and pretend to think it over while staying completely silent. They may entice your interviewer to increase the range.
- If you are familiar with someone in high places, do not be afraid to ask them to be one of your references. They may just be the ones to help you get the job.

CHAPTER 7 HIGHLIGHTS

Chapter 7 – Part 1:

- During a phone interview, if you find yourself in an uneasy situation, kindly ask your interviewer to hold until you can resolve your issue.
- A Call Wall is the best way to keep all of your interviewing information neat and organized. Keep information for each company together and separated from the other companies. Also make sure that your Call Wall is in a Quiet Zone. Lock yourself in a room if you have to. The last thing you need is an interruption when you are in the middle of an interview.

Chapter 7 – Part 2:

- Even after receiving several offers, it is necessary to continue looking for other job offers. There may be something better out there.
- Avoid interview fashion no-nos. Make sure your shoes are always clean. It seems weird, but shoes are one of the first things employers look at, so make sure clean and polished. Men, avoid flashy ties. Save them for when you become Senior Manager. Also, match shoes, suit, and belt colors. Women, match bag to shoes and, if applicable, belt.
- On the day of the interview: Allow extra time in your transportation schedule in case anything unforeseen comes up. If you arrive early, you can always sit in the parking lot, reviewing your S.C.A.R.F. stories, until the time of your appointment.

Chapter 7 – Part 3:

- Remember to treat gatekeepers (receptionists, custodians, security guards, etc.) with respect. You never know who might have a say in the hiring process.
- Even when the pressure is on in the interview, don't forget to use techniques such as the Relaxation, Mirror Matching, and Maverick Follow-Up Techniques.

- Don't feel bad for rejecting an offer, especially if you have better offers lined up. You have to accept the position that best matches your ideal job criterion.

- During the interview: Don't forget to sit at a 45-degree angle away from your interviewer. Once you begin discussing serious matters, change positions so that you are facing them straight on. They will understand now that you are engaged.

- If the company you are interviewing with supports the same causes and/or efforts as you, let them know. They like to you know that they are dealing with like-minded candidates.

- Remember to include moments of silence throughout your interview. It makes sure the interviewer is paying attention and keeps them on their toes, wanting more.

CHAPTER 8 HIGHLIGHTS

Chapter 8 – Part 1:

- Do not get terribly bogged down if rejected from a position. See it as an opportunity to start over again and improve your skills.
- Use your contacts to your advantage, just so long as you don't become a nuisance.
- "Don't give up" is easy to say, but hard to put into practice. Take this piece of advice to heart and you may be surprised what comes your way.

Chapter 8 – Part 2:

- Don't be afraid to write a letter to an employer asking them to reconsider their decision or search for an alternative. Be sure to reiterate your main selling points from the interview. You may just be able to sway their opinion.
- What is your target? Is it a long shot? It doesn't have to be. Find a way to achieve your goal in the shortest amount of time and with the least amount of resistance.
- During the last term of your senior year, remember that things will get hectic. Your grades may suffer as a result of your increased responsibilities. Strive at the beginning of the term to do your best, so that, if your grades do falter, you will have a safety net.

Chapter 8 – Part 3:

- If a job offer requires a move, consider the pros and cons of relocating. Is the new city the right fit for you? Will it be easy to visit family? If the answers to these questions are favorable, make the move.
- You've got to do whatever works, and that almost always means scrapping the old ways of finding a job and doing things you're not used to or that seem crazy at first.
- Job searching can be a stressful experience. Be sure to take a break from your search here and there to prevent any problems in your relationships and friendships.

WHAT'S NEXT?

The job-hunting advice presented in this book is only the tip of the iceberg. I wanted to include much more on resume writing, but couldn't due to space limitations. That's why I created the Resume Transformation training program to help you gain an unfair advantage over the competition by learning how to write your resume just as good if not BETTER than so called "professional" resume writers. In this course, you'll learn my step-by-step system for writing resumes that has taken me YEARS to perfect.

To learn more about this revolutionary training program, watch my promotional video at www.ResumeTransformationBlog.com.

See you on the other side!

—Landon

ABOUT THE AUTHORS

Landon Long is an ex-recruiter and the founder of InterviewMaster-Mind.com. Landon has screened several thousands of job seekers for one of the top 10 largest staffing and recruiting agencies in the U.S. As an author, marketer, resume expert and interview coach, Landon has helped hundreds of job seekers in all different types of industries. His methods have been tested in some of the toughest screening environments (i.e. Fortune 100 and 500 corporations) and they've also been used by some of the top job seekers in the country.

Prior to being an interview coach, Landon's professional background was in online marketing for one of the largest life insurance brokerage firms in the US; and project management for a $2.2 billion per year commercial real-estate developer where he's interviewed and screened over 95 multi-million dollar companies as his primary undertaking.

Jesse Stretch is a full time writer from Richmond, Virginia. His contact information, as well as information concerning his other projects, can be found at www.JesseStretch.com. Jesse is a true A-Player and is always eager to take on new assignments. Contact him with your proposal or idea today.

Made in the USA
Charleston, SC
15 November 2013